What God Is Like

Transformational Theology 1

Malcolm Webber

Published by:

Strategic Press
www.StrategicPress.org

Strategic Press is a division of Strategic Global Assistance, Inc.
www.sgai.org

513 S. Main St. Suite 2
Elkhart, IN 46516
U.S.A.

+1-844-532-3371 (+1-844-LEADER-1)

ISBN: 978-1-888810-72-1

All Scripture references are from the English Standard Version (ESV) of the Bible, unless otherwise indicated.

Contents

Preface

Paul says that when we *look at God* we are changed by His Spirit into His image.

> *And we all, with unveiled face, beholding the glory of the Lord, are being transformed into the same image from one degree of glory to another. For this comes from the Lord who is the Spirit.* (2 Corinthians 3:18)

It is our hope and prayer that God will use this writing and the associated learning designs to help multitudes of men, women and children around the world to do this – to look at God, to see Him clearly and to be transformed more and more into His image!

Malcolm Webber, Ph.D.
January 1, 2024

Endorsements

"This is the best book I've ever read on what God is like. It reveals God and introduces Him to us with clarity, purity and transformational power! It has brought me into a deep encounter with God. As I read through its truth and meditate on each of the characteristics of God, I can't help but spontaneously worship from the depths of my heart. All through the teachings of this book, I and many other leaders have exclaimed, 'Every truth about God is so profoundly and directly relevant to us! It's life to us!' Yes! It is life, not mere theory! It is powerful, not just dry knowledge. I pray that it will refresh every one of its readers in our personal knowledge of God, connect us deeply to God – the Foundation of our life – and enable us to walk in His power for the fulfilling of His great purposes, for the glory of His name!" (Church Leader, East Asia)

"These teachings have offered me a unique opportunity to study theology and the attributes of God from a different perspective. Unlike my previous educational experiences, which were focused on rote learning, these teachings emphasized practical application. God's love and goodness have had a profound impact on my life!" (Church Leader, Africa)

"I'm currently studying for a doctorate in theology, but for the first time through your teaching, I'm touching on a different theology that changes not only my thoughts and teaching, but my entire life, including my circle of influence in the world and the Church, and the greatest deepening of my spiritual life toward God and my experiences. This teaching leads me to a new change in my life." (Church Leader, North Africa)

"I have been using *Transformational Theology* in my own life to build my trust and dependency on God. I have also used this to teach my church and it has brought the church members to the feet of Jesus in repentance. It is amazing how the lives of the members are being transformed – their union with Christ has greatly improved and relationships between members are growing deeper. Families are now using the teachings in their homes and great testimonies are coming out of it." (Church Leader, Africa)

"When I encountered this teaching, I felt like crying for joy because of the realities I was discovering about the Lord. I thought to myself, 'How is it possible that I have been a believer walking with the Lord for years, and there are still things I am not aware of about God?' It was as if it were the first time I had learned about these truths, even though I had read them many times before. I am so joyful to know how much compassion God has towards us. I praise the Lord for *Transformational Theology*, and thank all of you for blessing us with this impactful ministry." (Church Leader, Africa)

"Even though I have studied the attributes of God and knew them well, the simplicity of this teaching and the transformational implications took me to a completely different dimension in my walk with God." (Church Leader, Middle East)

"After learning about 'God is Love' in *Transformational Theology* I have been thinking about sharing and showing God's love to my neighbors. One of the young girls I know is blind and neglected. I now visit with her each week and take her to church. This has had a huge impact on her life!" (Church Leader, Middle East)

"The teaching on 'God is Personal' in *Transformational Theology* has had a major impact in my life. This is the first time I have experienced the joy of the Holy Spirit over this very personal relationship. I have had bad experiences with leaders in the church and as I went through this training I heard the affirming voice of God telling me I am beautiful and He has a special place in His heart for me. I was so touched to learn that He cares deeply about me personally." (Church Leader, Middle East)

"Through *Transformational Theology*, we came to the realization that our previous understanding of God was limited and often incorrect. We tried to handle things on our own, only turning to God for the larger challenges. This approach led to many failures, but through this training God brought us to repentance. Now, each of us is practicing reliance on God for our current challenges, so we can truly experience God's Presence in our lives." (Church Leader, East Asia)

"In the past, when I faced adversity, I doubted God's love. Learning that God is Light through this training has made it clearer to me that God is faithful, without deceit. Because of this, I have repented and now seek to guard my life carefully!" (Church Leader, East Asia)

"I heard of the truth that 'God is Omniscient' early in my faith but never deeply experienced God's omniscience until I went through *Transformational Theology*. God's knowledge is infinite and immeasurable. Even in adversity, discouragement, weakness, or failure, what do I experience that He doesn't know about? He has numbered the hairs on my head; He knows every word on my tongue, and my thoughts and intentions are open before Him. The Lord knows my experiences, which is a great comfort. In the Presence of an all-knowing God, I don't need to hide anything and can freely pour out my heart to Him, whether in joy or sorrow, trouble or confusion. Knowing that He is omniscient, I am more willing to submit to God's guidance and rely solely on Him." (Church Leader, East Asia)

Introduction

What is your view of God? What do you think He is like?

Many Christians hold wrong views of God. Here are some of them:

- God is a heavenly policeman who is constantly looking for opportunities to punish those who break His law.
- God is a heavenly grandfather who expects nothing from us but is always ready to spoil us and meet our every desire.
- God is a heavenly clock builder who wound up the universe like a clock and since then is letting it run, without any direct personal involvement.
- God is a heavenly schoolmaster who prizes academic achievements.
- God is a heavenly psychologist whose greatest desire is that we feel good emotionally.
- God is a heavenly impresario who loves to inspire and attend big, dramatic events and moving music concerts.
- God is a heavenly technician who has established various formulas that we are to discover from the Bible and then use to get whatever we want.
- God is a heavenly dictator who arbitrarily decides what happens in the world.
- God is a playful power who toys with us and tries to trick us.
- God is an obsessive nitpicker who requires absolute perfection from us or else He will be disappointed.
- God is exceedingly religious, requiring that we follow many detailed ceremonies and rituals in order to please Him.

- God is the managing director of the universe, guiding all events but without much hands-on personal involvement.
- God is an irritable parent, some days in a bad mood and others in a good one.
- God is a meek and gentle servant who accepts everyone just as they are with no expectations at all, always ready to help.
- God is a smoldering ball of wrath, ready at any moment to break forth and destroy us.
- God is an impersonal force who rules the universe and to whom we must submit.
- God has a vague existence, as if He were a spiritual mist floating somewhere above the earth.
- God is a being so far off and so unlike man that He is entirely unapproachable and distant.
- God is a being who exists in some way, but everyone can have their own personal and valid view of who or what "God" is.
- God is a being who is always changing: growing and developing like the rest of the changing universe.
- God is everything and everything is God.

As we can see, there are so many wrong views that people have of God!

These and other false conceptions of God need to be corrected if our spiritual lives are to have any real meaning and depth.

As created beings, it is easy for us to have a very small view of God or to understand Him only in human terms or in terms of the people we have known and the experiences we have had. It is only as we look deeply at what God says about Himself in His Word that we can begin to have an accurate picture of who He is and what He is like. We need God to reveal Himself to us through His Word by His Spirit.

As we now look at each of the many characteristics of God, we will see God more clearly, we will understand Him more truly, and we will find a deeper place of union with Him! By God's grace, may our experience be the same as Job's!

> *I had heard of You by the hearing of the ear, but now my eye sees You ...* (Job 42:5)

Summary

We will sum up many of God's characteristics under five major categories:

1. **God is Spirit**
    - God is self-existent
    - God is eternal
    - God is independent
    - God is invisible
    - God is constant

2. **God is infinite**
    - God is everywhere
    - God is all-knowing
    - God is all-powerful

3. **God is love**
    - God is personal
    - God is good
    - God is gracious
    - God is beautiful

4. **God is light**
    - God is truth
    - God is wise
    - God is holy
    - God is righteous and just

5. **God is glorious**

Transformational Implications:

- Because God is One, each of these characteristics is a quality of the entire triune God. So, for example, the Son of God and the Holy Spirit are infinite in Presence, knowledge and power. We should not limit God in any way.
- Because God is so great and magnificent in every way, we are brought to our knees in humility before Him.

> *Then Job answered the LORD and said: "I know that You can do all things, and that no purpose of Yours can be thwarted. 'Who is this that hides counsel without knowledge?' Therefore I have uttered what I did not understand, things too wonderful for me, which I did not know. 'Hear, and I will speak; I will question You, and You make it known to me.' I had heard of You by the hearing of the ear, but now my eye sees You; therefore I despise myself, and repent in dust and ashes."* (Job 42:1-6)

God Is Spirit

God Is Spirit

> *God is Spirit, and those who worship Him must worship in spirit and truth.* (John 4:24)

This refers to God's fundamental nature, His essence, His Being – He is "Spirit."

It is very difficult to describe the nature of God's Being as Spirit. It is easier to define Him by what He is *not*. God is not created and is not subject to time or space. As Spirit, God does not exist within our framework of time and space. He is entirely outside of it.

> *For thus says the One who is high and lifted up, who inhabits eternity* ... (Isaiah 57:15)
>
> *But who is able to build Him a house, since heaven, even highest heaven, cannot contain Him?* ... (2 Chronicles 2:6)

As Spirit, God has a kind of existence that is nothing like anything we know of or can possibly understand.

We are made of skin, blood, nerves and many other things, and we have arms, legs, organs and many parts. Everything we know has parts; for example, a tree has leaves, roots and bark. But God is not made out of anything, and He has no parts.

We also have dimensions – we weigh a certain amount and are of a particular height. But God has no dimensions. He is infinite Spirit.

Furthermore, everything in the material world can be destroyed; people can get sick and die, and their houses can burn down. But God cannot be destroyed. He cannot be harmed. In addition, everything we know continually changes, but God never changes.

Everything we know in the material world is subject to time. But God is not. He is outside of time. He sees everything at once – past, present and future.

Moreover, He is outside of space. Everything we know is subject to space. If one thing occupies a certain place, then something else cannot occupy that same space at the same time. For us to be somewhere else requires us to move there. But God is not subject to space. He never needs to go anywhere to be there. All of Him is everywhere at the same time!

Consequently, God does not have any form that we could understand. He is pure, eternal, infinite, uncreated Spirit.

Sometimes people say that "God is *a* spirit." This is not accurate and is quite misleading. This implies that He is like other "spirits" such as angels or demons. God is not like them. He is their Creator also. His nature is other than theirs just as His nature is other than ours. God is not one of many spirits; His nature is entirely unique.

As eternal Spirit, God has life – eternal life, infinite life. He is the uncreated One, the Living God.

> *But the Lord is the true God; He is the living God and the everlasting King ...* (Jeremiah 10:10)
>
> *For as the Father has life in Himself, so He has granted the Son also to have life in Himself.* (John 5:26)

In John 5:26, Jesus said that God "has life in Himself." This is because of His nature as infinite Spirit. In contrast, we do not have life in ourselves. We, and every other created thing, are entirely dependent on God for our ongoing existence.

> *For from Him and through Him and to Him are all things. To Him be glory forever. Amen.* (Romans 11:36)

But God Himself is dependent upon no one else and nothing else. He "has life in Himself."

Moreover, His infinite life is the Source of all life. He Himself is the "Fountain of Life."

> *For with You is the fountain of life; in Your light do we see light.* (Psalm 36:9)

The nature of God as Spirit is not just an abstract, philosophical idea. This truth has profound transformational implications.

One major implication relates to idolatry. In both testaments, the living God is frequently contrasted with the false gods, which are nothing but dead objects of wood, metal or stone.

> *But the Lord is the true God; He is the living God and the everlasting King. At His wrath the earth quakes, and the nations cannot endure His indignation. Thus shall you say to them: "The gods who did not make the heavens and the earth shall perish from the earth and from under the heavens."* (Jeremiah 10:10-11)

How foolish it is for people to worship man-made idols of wood or stone, or to worship the idol of money, when we have been given the privilege of worshiping the true God – the uncreated, infinite God who is Spirit!

> *... every goldsmith is put to shame by his idols, for his images are false, and there is no breath in them. They are worthless, a work of delusion ... Not like these is He who is the portion of Jacob, for He is the One who formed all things ...* (Jeremiah 51:17-19)

God commands us to turn from all idols and give our hearts entirely and only to Him!

> *For they themselves report concerning us the kind of reception we had among you, and how you turned to God from idols to serve the living and true God ...* (1 Thessalonians 1:9)

Because He is the only God, the true God, the living God, we worship Him. Significantly, when Jesus said, "God is Spirit" to the woman at the well in Samaria, the context was their discussion about where people should worship God.

> *"Our fathers worshiped on this mountain, but You say that in Jerusalem is the place where people ought to worship." Jesus said to her, "Woman, believe Me, the hour is coming when neither on this mountain nor in Jerusalem will you worship the Father ... But the hour is coming, and is now here, when the true worshipers will worship the Father in spirit and truth, for the Father is seeking such people to worship Him. God is Spirit, and those who worship Him must worship in spirit and truth."* (John 4:20-21, 23-24)

Jesus told her that the true worship of God that "is coming, and is now here" will not require one to be present either in Jerusalem or Samaria. True worship will not be about physical location. After Jesus' resurrection and the coming of the Holy Spirit, Christ is in us!

> *Jesus answered him, "If anyone loves Me, he will keep My Word, and My Father will love him, and We will come to him and make Our home with him."* (John 14:23)
>
> *... so that Christ may dwell in your hearts through faith ...* (Ephesians 3:17)
>
> *... Christ in you, the hope of glory.* (Colossians 1:27)

Jesus said, "... the hour is coming, and is now here, when the true worshipers will worship the Father in spirit and truth ..." (John 4:23). This indicates that we now have a new way of worship. In the time of the Old Testament, God did require them to worship in a certain place and follow certain rituals. But it is different now. We do not need to go to a special place or follow certain rituals. Moreover, we should not introduce old Jewish ways of worship into the Church.[1] Instead, we should worship God in spirit and truth!

To worship God, we need merely to turn to Him and look at Him as He dwells in us by His Spirit. We can worship Him all day, at all times, whatever we are doing, whatever we are going through. Inwardly, in our hearts, we can look at Him, depend on Him, surrender to Him, love Him, worship Him!

> *For we are the [true] circumcision, who worship by the Spirit of God and glory in Christ Jesus and put no confidence in the flesh ... (Philippians 3:3)*

Amazingly, the Father is seeking such worshipers!

> *But the hour is coming, and is now here, when the true worshipers will worship the Father in spirit and truth, for the Father is seeking such people to worship Him. (John 4:23)*

And then, when we worship God together in His Church, we experience the fullness of God! Together we are His new temple – His dwelling place!

> *So then you are no longer strangers and aliens, but you are fellow citizens with the saints and members of the household of God, built on the foundation of the apostles and prophets, Christ Jesus Himself being the Cornerstone, in whom the whole structure, being joined together, grows into a holy temple in the Lord. In Him you also are being built together into a dwelling place for God by the Spirit. (Ephesians 2:19-22)*
>
> *... that according to the riches of His glory He may grant you to be strengthened with power through His Spirit in your inner being, so that Christ may dwell in your hearts through faith – that you, being*

---

1 For more on the relationship of the Christian to the Mosaic Law, please see *The Christian and the Law* by Malcolm Webber.

> *rooted and grounded in love, may have strength to comprehend with all the saints what is the breadth and length and height and depth, and to know the love of Christ that surpasses knowledge, that you may be filled with all the fullness of God.* (Ephesians 3:16-19)

Transformational Implications:

- Because God is Spirit, we must worship Him in spirit and truth.

  > *God is Spirit, and those who worship Him must worship in spirit and truth.* (John 4:24).
  >
  > *For we are the circumcision, who worship by the Spirit of God and glory in Christ Jesus and put no confidence in the flesh ...* (Philippians 3:3)

  To worship God "in spirit" means it is our joy and privilege to know Him, love Him and worship Him in our hearts where He dwells by His Spirit. It is not necessary to go anywhere special or perform certain outward rituals. Simply turn inwardly to Him, surrender to Him, trust Him, love Him, look at Him and worship Him!

  To worship God "in truth" means to worship "the true God" and not idols and other false gods (John 17:3; Romans 1:25; 1 John 5:20).

  To worship God "in truth" also means to put away sin and all untruth and worship Him in purity, holiness and integrity.

  Incredibly, "the Father is seeking such people to worship Him" (John 4:23)!

- Because God is the "Fountain of Life" (Psalm 36:9), our union with Him will be the Source of everything in our lives.

> *"Blessed is the man who trusts in the* Lord, *whose trust is the* Lord. *He is like a tree planted by water, that sends out its roots by the stream, and does not fear when heat comes, for its leaves remain green, and is not anxious in the year of drought, for it does not cease to bear fruit."* (Jeremiah 17:7-8)

God Is Self-Existent

A common question is, "If God created all things, who created God? Where did He come from?"

One of my earliest memories was when I was lying in bed one night – perhaps three or four years old – and I was thinking about God. I wondered, "If God created all things, then where did God come from?" I was puzzled and concerned by that. I had a desire to call out to my mother and ask her, but I did not. Instead, I lay in my bed wondering. Suddenly, the Presence of God came upon me, and I had a deep sense of peace and I knew that I did not need to answer this question.

In His Presence, I felt God's love for me, and I wanted to tell God that I loved Him too, but I was embarrassed. So, I hid under the blankets and then popped my head out to say, "I love You, God!" and then quickly pulled the blankets over my head again. I did this several times, experiencing the love and peace of God. I knew in my heart, that even though I did not know where God came from, it was alright!

Of course, God was never created. He was always there. God is self-existent and He did not come from anything. He is the uncaused Cause. He created everything but He had no beginning and there is nothing bigger than God from which He came or on which He depends. "Self-existence" means that God simply exists by Himself.

When God revealed Himself to Moses in the burning bush, He told Moses His Name:

> *God said to Moses, "I am who I am." And He said, "Say this to the people of Israel: 'I am has sent me to you.'"* (Exodus 3:14)

The Hebrew word translated "I am" is *ehyeh* (אֶהְיֶה). It is the first-person, masculine, singular form of the verb "to be." This is where the Hebrew name of God *Yahweh* comes from: it is the third-person, masculine, singular form of the same verb, and it means, essentially, "He is."

Moses asked God for His Name, and God responded with the verb "to be." Essentially, God said, "My Name is Existence ... Tell them the Self-Existent One has sent you"!

God exists without being created. He simply "is."

> *"I am the Alpha and the Omega," says the Lord God, "who is and who was and who is to come, the Almighty."* (Revelation 1:8)

God has always been and always will be.

In contrast, man does not have self-existence. No other being is self-existent. We and all created beings are entirely dependent on God for our continued existence. God holds all things together:

> *And He [the Son of God] is before all things, and in Him all things hold together.* (Colossians 1:17)
>
> *... He [the Son of God] upholds the universe by the Word of His power ...* (Hebrews 1:3; see also Nehemiah 9:6; Acts 17:25)

Everything depends on the Son of God for its continued existence. God, however, has life in Himself:

> *For as the Father has life in Himself, so He has granted the Son also to have life in Himself.* (John 5:26)

God's self-existence also means that He exists from and for Himself. All of His works are according to His own will and for the ultimate purpose of His own glory.

> *For from Him and through Him and to Him are all things. To Him be glory forever. Amen.* (Romans 11:36)
>
> *... yet for us there is one God, the Father, from whom are all things and for whom we exist, and one Lord, Jesus Christ, through whom are all things and through whom we exist.* (1 Corinthians 8:6)

Because God is the only One with self-existence, therefore, everything that He does is for His own purposes. Everything is ultimately because of the will of God and then serves in the end to glorify God.

If a created being were to live from and for himself, that would be utter foolishness and terrible pride.[2] Our only purpose is to live for the One who created us – to do His will and to bring Him glory. There is no greater meaning than this!

> *For none of us lives to himself, and none of us dies to himself. For if we live, we live to the Lord, and if we die, we die to the Lord. So then, whether we live or whether we die, we are the Lord's.* (Romans 14:7-8)
>
> *So, whether you eat or drink, or whatever you do, do all to the glory of God.* (1 Corinthians 10:31)

Everything in our lives is from Him and for Him. We are utterly dependent upon God for everything, and the entire purpose of our lives is His glory. This is the highest calling we could possibly have!

<u>Transformational Implications:</u>

- Because God is self-existent and we are not, we are dependent on Him for everything!

---

2 This was the original sin of the devil (Isaiah 14:13-14).

> *And He is before all things, and in Him all things hold together.* (Colossians 1:17)

- Because God is self-existent, our only purpose is to live for the One who created us – to do His will and to bring Him glory. There is no higher purpose than that!

> *... even as He chose us in Him before the foundation of the world, that we should be holy and blameless before Him. In love He predestined us for adoption to Himself as sons through Jesus Christ, according to the purpose of His will, to the praise of His glorious grace, with which He has blessed us in the Beloved ... so that we who were the first to hope in Christ might be to the praise of His glory ...* [the Holy Spirit] *is the guarantee of our inheritance until we acquire possession of it, to the praise of His glory.* (Ephesians 1:4-6, 12, 14)

God is Eternal

Because God is self-existent, He is therefore eternal. He had no beginning, and He will have no end.

> *Before the mountains were brought forth, or ever You had formed the earth and the world, from everlasting to everlasting You are God.* (Psalm 90:2)

God is "from everlasting" – He had no beginning. God is "to everlasting" – He will have no end.

> *Thus says the Lord, the King of Israel and his Redeemer, the Lord of hosts: "I am the first and I am the last; besides Me there is no god ..."* (Isaiah 44:6)
>
> *"... I am the Alpha and the Omega, the first and the last, the beginning and the end."* (Revelation 22:13)

Man's existence is entirely dependent on God; therefore, man had a beginning when God chose to create him. But because God is dependent on nothing, He always was.

God's eternity does not merely mean that He lives for a long time. It means He exists entirely outside of time. He "inhabits eternity"!

> *For thus says the One who is high and lifted up, who inhabits eternity, whose Name is Holy ...* (Isaiah 57:15)

Before Creation, there was no time. When God created the world in the beginning, He created time. Therefore, He is not subject to time. He is not waiting to see what will happen tomorrow, and He is not trying to remember what happened a long time ago; God sees all things throughout all history at once.

For us, our lives are a series of moments of time. But there is no succession of moments for Him; everything is "now" for God. Of course, this is impossible for us to comprehend because we exist entirely within the realm of time, but it does help us to appreciate Moses' and Peter's words:

> *For a thousand years in Your sight are but as yesterday when it is past, or as a watch in the night.* (Psalm 90:4)
>
> *But do not overlook this one fact, beloved, that with the Lord one day is as a thousand years, and a thousand years as one day.* (2 Peter 3:8)

Peter was not specifically connecting a day with 1000 years. He could just as well have said, "With the Lord, one hour is as 5000 years and 5000 years as one hour." God is outside of time. He is not subject to time. He sees everything all at once.

In our minds and memories, what happened last week or last year recedes into a distant and vague past. But God sees everything at all times with perfect clarity and vividness. Nothing is past to Him, and nothing is future. It is all present.

God exists outside of time. Thus, He is not limited by time and He, unlike us, is not changed by the passing of time. He is no older today than He was a thousand years ago.

Of course, God understands His created world and He knows that, from our perspective, things happen in the realm of time. In the created world, there is past, present and future. Things happen in succession and not all at once. Consequently, God is said to act at certain times; for example:

> *But when the fullness of time had come, God sent forth His Son ...* (Galatians 4:4)

In a manner of speaking, God watches the events of history unfold and then, at certain points in time, He acts. Both perspectives are true – God is outside of time, and He acts in different ways inside time. He is the Lord of time.

The truth that God is eternal has many profound transformational implications.

Because God is the Lord of time, we will commit our past and all its pain and regret to Him.

> *... But one thing I do: forgetting what lies behind and straining forward to what lies ahead ...* (Philippians 3:13)
>
> *... casting all your anxieties on Him, because He cares for you.* (1 Peter 5:7)

We do not have to figure our past out. In reality, we cannot figure it out; there is so much in our lives we do not understand.

Moreover, we do not have to "fix" our past. In fact, we cannot fix our past. For all of us, there is so much in our past that we wish we could go back and change, but we cannot. Instead, we must commit the past to the One who is the Lord of time and leave it in His hands.

Sometimes we do not let go of our past. We hold onto it and it overwhelms us. The brokenness of the past can destroy our hope for the future. We must look at God and give Him the past, and then leave it with Him.

As Paul says, "... forgetting what lies behind and straining forward to what lies ahead." Holding the past in our own hands is an expression of our own trust in ourselves. Even though we cannot fix anything, we still wish we could, and that is why we keep thinking about the past. We must give up that control and, instead, commit the past to God.

We might pray something like this to God:

> *Lord, even though from my side, if I think about the past, all I see is pain and brokenness, trouble and errors, and failures. But I'm going to trust You! Even though it makes no sense to me, I trust that You had purpose, You had design. Somehow, You were in control of everything in my life.*
>
> *And so I choose to let go of the pain, the brokenness, and the regret. Then the chains of the past are broken. And I'm able now to march boldly forward into the future no longer weighed down by regret. With a strong faith in God, I am free from the brokenness of the past.*

Of course, if there are things that we did in the past that we still need to make right – either with God or with others – then we need to do that. But we must cast the brokenness of it all onto God.

Moreover, because God is the Lord of time, we will also trust God for the future. He holds it all in His hands.

> *For I know the plans I have for you, declares the* LORD, *plans for welfare and not for evil, to give you a future and a hope.* (Jeremiah 29:11)

Unlike us, God has no regrets about the past and no fears or anxieties about the future! And this great God who is the Lord of time, cares for us. He holds our lives in His hands, in His loving, caring, protecting hands. He holds our past, our present, and our future in His hands. So we can cast our regrets for the past and our anxieties for the future on Him. We can cast every part of our lives – past, present and future – on Him.

In addition, because God is eternal, He is never taken by surprise, nor does He need to make contingency plans. Consequently, as we trust Him, we will have peace and hope, irrespective of what happens. We know that He is always in control and that He will, in the end, fulfill His great purposes.

> *And we know that for those who love God all things work together for good, for those who are called according to His purpose.* (Romans 8:28)
>
> *... The Lord is at hand; do not be anxious about anything, but in everything by prayer and supplication with thanksgiving let your requests be made known to God. And the peace of God, which surpasses all understanding, will guard your hearts and your minds in Christ Jesus.* (Philippians 4:5-7)

From our side, we are regularly taken by surprise. We find ourselves in situations that we had not planned on. In those times we must look at God – the eternal God – the One who is always in control. Then we will have peace, knowing that God is working out His great eternal purposes. We will let go of the anxiety, and the peace of God will guard our hearts and minds.

Finally, because God is outside of time and sees everything past, present and future, we will recognize the significance of generational succession to Him, and we will work hard to pass the treasures of His life, truth, grace, character and vision from one generation to the next.

> *Know therefore that the LORD your God is God, the faithful God who keeps covenant and steadfast love with those who love Him and keep His commandments, to a thousand generations ...* (Deuteronomy 7:9)
>
> *For the LORD is good; His steadfast love endures forever, and His faithfulness to all generations.* (Psalm 100:5)

The younger generation will understand the past, honor the past and intentionally build on the past, while the older generation will share the past, trust God for the future, and intentionally build and empower the next generation.[3]

---

3 For more on generational succession, please see *LeaderStream: A Generational Stream of Life, Truth, Vision and Leadership Succession* by Malcolm Webber.

> *Remember your leaders, those who spoke to you the Word of God. Consider the outcome of their way of life, and imitate their faith. Jesus Christ is the same yesterday and today and forever.* (Hebrews 13:7-8)

Transformational Implications:

- Because God is the Lord of time, we will commit our past and all its pain and regret to Him.

  > *... But one thing I do: forgetting what lies behind and straining forward to what lies ahead ...* (Philippians 3:13)

- Because God is the Lord of time, we will also trust God for the future. He holds it all in His hands.

  > *For I know the plans I have for you, declares the Lord, plans for welfare and not for evil, to give you a future and a hope.* (Jeremiah 29:11)

- Because God is eternal, He is never taken by surprise, nor does He need to make contingency plans. Consequently, as we trust Him, we will have peace and hope, irrespective of what happens. We know that He is always in control and that He will, in the end, fulfill His great purposes.

  > *And we know that for those who love God all things work together for good, for those who are called according to His purpose.* (Romans 8:28)

- Because God is outside of time and sees everything past, present and future, we will recognize the significance of generational succession to Him, and we will work hard to pass the treasures of His life, truth, grace, character and vision from one generation to the next.

  > *Know therefore that the Lord your God is God, the faithful God who keeps covenant and steadfast love with those who*

> *love Him and keep His commandments, to a thousand generations ... (Deuteronomy 7:9)*

God Is Independent

Because God is self-existent, He is also therefore "independent."

> *Who has first given to Me, that I should repay him? Whatever is under the whole heaven is Mine.* (Job 41:11)

No one has ever given to God anything that God did not first give him. We are entirely dependent on Him, but He is dependent on nothing outside of Himself.

The independence of God has many transformational implications. First, it breaks the power of idolatry.

> *... The God who made the world and everything in it, being Lord of heaven and earth, does not live in temples made by man, nor is He served by human hands, as though He needed anything, since He Himself gives to all mankind life and breath and everything.* (Acts 17:24-25)

Paul told the Athenians that God doesn't need anyone or anything. The Greeks had many gods – idols. Those idols were entirely dependent on man – for everything! They needed man to make them in the first place out of wood or stone. Then they needed man to take them from place to place. Man had to bring them money and food. The idols were completely dependent on man.

But the true God, in dramatic contrast, doesn't need anyone or anything. He Himself is the Source of life and everything for all.

Thus, the truth of God's independence breaks the power of idolatry. Paul was not merely discussing some abstract philosophical idea here. His teaching was deeply practical. Paul's purpose was that they would turn from serving dead idols who rely on them to serving the true living God.

Then, the independence of God brings us to humility:

> *But who am I, and what is my people, that we should be able thus to offer willingly? For all things come from You, and of Your own have we given You.* (1 Chronicles 29:14)

The independence of God, in 1 Chronicles 29, brought David to a deep humility and a gratefulness that he and the people were able to give to God with generosity and joy.

Next, the independence of God leads us to lives of righteousness:

> *"I will not accept a bull from your house or goats from your folds. For every beast of the forest is Mine, the cattle on a thousand hills. I know all the birds of the hills, and all that moves in the field is Mine. If I were hungry, I would not tell you, for the world and its fullness are Mine. Do I eat the flesh of bulls or drink the blood of goats? Offer to God a sacrifice of thanksgiving, and perform your vows to the Most High, and call upon Me in the day of trouble; I will deliver you, and you shall glorify Me."* (Psalm 50:9-15)

In Psalm 50, God says, in effect, "I don't need your sacrifices and offerings" (verses 8-9), "so bring Me, instead, lives of righteousness and integrity, not just outward forms."

In addition, the independence of God leads us to faith in Him and worship of Him:

> *"Or who has given a gift to Him that He might be repaid?" For from Him and through Him and to Him are all things. To Him be glory forever. Amen.* (Romans 11:35-36)

In the earlier chapters of Romans, Paul had demonstrated how absolutely lost everyone is apart from God's grace. Then, at the end of Chapter 11, he leads us to worship this great God – the One who is independent of all and who gives us His salvation freely. We are entirely dependent on God for everything – for life, and for eternal salvation – yet God needs nothing; He Himself is the Source of all. Therefore, we must trust Him and worship Him!

Also, the independence of God brings us to a place of unity in the Church:

> *... What do you have that you did not receive? If then you received it, why do you boast as if you did not receive it?* (1 Corinthians 4:7)

In the previous passages of 1 Corinthians, Paul had corrected the believers for their divisions. Each group was declaring the superiority of their own chosen leader (Paul, Apollos, Peter and even Christ). Paul now says, "God is the One who has given you everything – including your leaders. And He has given all these leaders to all of you. There is nothing special about you. It's all from God. Therefore, stop your boasting about one leader or the other!" In this way, the independence of God leads us to humility and also unity within the Church.

Furthermore, because God is independent, He does not need our fellowship or love. Some people think that God created man because He was lonely, and He needed man's fellowship or love. This is not true. God is not fortunate to have us. We are the fortunate ones to have Him!

God was fully satisfied – in fact, He was delighted – in Himself for all eternity in the fellowship of the triune God.

> *Father, I desire that they also, whom You have given Me, may be with Me where I am, to see My glory that You have given Me because You loved Me before the foundation of the world.* (John 17:24)

God has no unmet needs or desires. He is completely fulfilled in Himself. It is not just that God *does not* need man or the created world for anything; God *could not* need His creation for anything. He has no limitation, no lack, no deficiency of any kind.

This is what it means to be "blessed" – to be happy in a very rich sense. God is eternally and fully "blessed." He is happy!

> *... which He will display at the proper time – He who is the blessed and only Sovereign, the King of kings and Lord of lords ...* (1 Timothy 6:15)
>
> *... in accordance with the Gospel of the glory of the blessed God with which I have been entrusted.* (1 Timothy 1:11)

God is blessed because He delights in Himself.

Moreover, since He needs nothing outside of Himself, God has perfect freedom. He does whatever He wants.

> *Our God is in the heavens; He does all that He pleases.* (Psalm 115:3)

However, God's independence does not make us meaningless. Some may think if God does not need us for anything, then we have no importance at all. The fact is that God created us for His glory and purposes. He created us to freely choose to know Him, to willingly love Him, to serve Him from the heart. He made us to be eternally and exclusively satisfied by Him. That is our meaning and there is no greater meaning than this!

The incredible reality is that God chooses to delight in us.

> *You shall be a crown of beauty in the hand of the Lord, and a royal diadem in the hand of your God. ... the Lord delights in you ... and as the bridegroom rejoices over the bride, so shall your God rejoice over you.* (Isaiah 62:3-5)
>
> *The Lord your God is in your midst, a Mighty One who will save; He will rejoice over you with gladness; He will quiet you by His love; He will exult over you with loud singing.* (Zephaniah 3:17)

Because of His love and purpose, we have extraordinary value! God gives us this value.

Thus, rather than thinking that God finds His fulfillment in us in some way, we must find our entire fulfillment in God and God alone. When we do that, we will find our fullest meaning, our greatest joy, and our highest purpose.

> *In Him we have obtained an inheritance, having been predestined according to the purpose of Him who works all things according to the counsel of His will, so that we who were the first to hope in Christ might be to the praise of His glory.* (Ephesians 1:11-12)

Once again, the independence of God delivers us from pride and brings us to a deep place of humility, to surrender and dependence on God, and to great joy knowing that in Him we have great value and purpose.

<u>Transformational Implications:</u>

- Because God is independent, the bondage of idolatry is broken and we are free to choose to worship the true and living God.

  > *... The God who made the world and everything in it, being Lord of heaven and earth, does not live in temples made by man, nor is He served by human hands, as though He needed anything, since He Himself gives to all mankind life and breath and everything.* (Acts 17:24-25)

- Because God is independent, we respond to Him with humility and gratefulness that we are able to freely give to Him generously and joyfully.

  > *But who am I, and what is my people, that we should be able thus to offer willingly? For all things come from You, and of Your own have we given You.* (1 Chronicles 29:14)

- Because God is independent and needs nothing from us, our focus shifts from more ceremonial offerings to Him to giving Him the true worship of our lives of righteousness and integrity.

> *I will not accept a bull from your house or goats from your folds. For every beast of the forest is Mine, the cattle on a thousand hills. I know all the birds of the hills, and all that moves in the field is Mine. "If I were hungry, I would not tell you, for the world and its fullness are Mine. Do I eat the flesh of bulls or drink the blood of goats? Offer to God a sacrifice of thanksgiving, and perform your vows to the Most High, and call upon Me in the day of trouble; I will deliver you, and you shall glorify Me."* (Psalm 50:9-15)

- Because God is independent and we are entirely dependent on Him for everything – for life and for eternal salvation – we trust Him and worship Him with all our hearts!

> *"Or who has given a gift to Him that He might be repaid?" For from Him and through Him and to Him are all things. To Him be glory forever. Amen.* (Romans 11:35-36)

- Because God is independent and He has given us everything – including one another in the Church – we will love and accept one another in unity.

> *... What do you have that you did not receive? If then you received it, why do you boast as if you did not receive it?* (1 Corinthians 4:7)

- Because God is independent, we will not follow the error that God created us because He was lonely or needed us. Instead of thinking that God finds His fulfillment in us in some way, we will find our entire fulfillment in God and God alone. When we do that, we will find our fullest meaning, our greatest joy, and our highest purpose.

> *When all things are subjected to Him, then the Son Himself will also be subjected to Him who put all things in subjection under Him, that God may be all in all.* (1 Corinthians 15:28)

At the same time, even though God did not need us, He created us in such a way that He does enjoy us! Incredibly, the God who needs nothing is pleased with our lives, our love and our worship.

> *Finally, then, brothers, we ask and urge you in the Lord Jesus, that as you received from us how you ought to walk and to please God, just as you are doing, that you do so more and more.* (1 Thessalonians 4:1)

God Is Invisible

God does not have any form as created things do. Unless He reveals Himself, we cannot see Him, or know Him.

> *To the King of the ages, immortal, invisible, the only God, be honor and glory forever and ever. Amen.* (1 Timothy 1:17; see also Exodus 33:20; John 1:18; Romans 1:20; Colossians 1:15; 1 Timothy 6:16; Hebrews 11:27; 1 John 4:12)

As Spirit, God exists in a way entirely beyond what we know in the created world – it is not merely that we cannot see Him with our natural eyes.

If it were possible for a man to become invisible, then we would no longer see him, but we could still bump into him. But this is not what it means for God to be invisible. It is a bigger idea than that we simply cannot see God. It means that His entire existence is beyond anything that we understand or know in this natural created world. Consequently, unless God reveals Himself, we will not "bump into Him." He is Spirit. He is fundamentally different from us. This is why so many otherwise highly intelligent people do not believe in God – they cannot "see" Him. Man will never find God through his own learning or efforts – unless He reveals Himself, we cannot know Him.

> *"... no one knows who the Son is except the Father, or who the Father is except the Son and anyone to whom the Son chooses to reveal Him."* (Luke 10:22)

Because God is invisible He prohibits us from making images of Him. In the Law of Moses, the prohibition against making images of God was given specifically because God does not have any form. Therefore, it is wrong for man to try to make any likeness of Him.

> *You shall not make for yourself a carved image, or any likeness of anything that is in heaven above, or that is in the earth beneath, or that is in the water under the earth.* (Exodus 20:4)
>
> *Therefore watch yourselves very carefully. Since you saw no form on the day that the Lord spoke to you at Horeb out of the midst of the fire, beware lest you act corruptly by making a carved image for yourselves, in the form of any figure, the likeness of male or female, the likeness of any animal that is on the earth, the likeness of any winged bird that flies in the air, the likeness of anything that creeps on the ground, the likeness of any fish that is in the water under the earth. And beware lest you raise your eyes to heaven, and when you see the sun and the moon and the stars, all the host of heaven, you be drawn away and bow down to them and serve them, things that the Lord your God has allotted to all the peoples under the whole heaven.* (Deuteronomy 4:15-19)

At certain times in the Old Testament, God revealed Himself to people in a human form (Genesis 18:1-2) or in other forms such as the burning bush (Exodus 3:2) or the pillar of cloud and pillar of fire (Exodus 13:21). But those were temporary manifestations in forms that God chose. The people did not see His eternal nature as Spirit.

But then, incredibly, when Jesus came, He perfectly revealed the invisible God to man:

> *No one has ever seen God; the only God, who is at the Father's side, He has made Him known.* (John 1:18)

John says that while no one has ever seen God, yet in the Lord Jesus, we *have* seen God!

> *That which was from the beginning, which we have heard, which we have seen with our eyes, which we looked upon and have touched with our hands, concerning the Word of Life – the Life was made manifest, and we have seen it, and testify to it and proclaim to you the eternal Life, which was with the Father and was made manifest*

> *to us – that which we have seen and heard we proclaim also to you, so that you too may have fellowship with us; and indeed our fellowship is with the Father and with His Son Jesus Christ.* (1 John 1:1-3)

Not only the early disciples experienced God in Jesus, but we can too. In the Lord Jesus, we can see God, we can hear Him, we can touch Him, we can know Him.

> *... Whoever has seen Me has seen the Father ...* (John 14:9)
>
> *... in these last days He has spoken to us by His Son ... He is the radiance of the glory of God and the exact imprint of His nature ...* (Hebrews 1:2-3)

God has revealed Himself in the Person of His Son. The Son of God is the exact expression of the nature of God. And now, in our hearts, the Holy Spirit reveals the Son of God to us! There is no need for us to be jealous of the early disciples who personally saw Jesus – Christ now dwells in us and we can deeply know Him too!

> *To them God chose to make known how great among the Gentiles are the riches of the glory of this mystery, which is Christ in you, the hope of glory.* (Colossians 1:27)
>
> *For God, who said, "Let light shine out of darkness," has shone in our hearts to give the light of the knowledge of the glory of God in the face of Jesus Christ.* (2 Corinthians 4:6; see also Matthew 11:27; Luke 10:22; John 17:26)

The Holy Spirit in us reveals the Son of God, in whom is the fullness of the triune God! Inwardly, we can look at Him, love Him, know Him. In the incarnation, the invisible God was perfectly revealed in the God-Man, the Lord Jesus. And now, by the Holy Spirit in us, the invisible God can be seen in our hearts as we turn to Him and look at Him. We can see the invisible God!

> *"Whoever has My commandments and keeps them, he it is who loves Me. And he who loves Me will be loved by My Father, and I will love him and manifest Myself to him."* (John 14:21)
>
> *For through Him we both have access in one Spirit to the Father.* (Ephesians 2:18)

This is why we do not need images of God. He is in us and as we turn to Him we can see Him.

This does not mean that Jesus in His humanity directly expressed God's infinite and invisible Being, but rather that He revealed God's character and nature.

Moreover, when we love one another, we too reveal God's character and love:

> *No one has ever seen God; if we love one another, God abides in us and His love is perfected in us.* (1 John 4:12)

Jesus perfectly revealed the Father to man. Then the Holy Spirit in our hearts reveals the Father and the Son to us. Now *we* reveal God, albeit imperfectly, to others! As we walk in union with Christ and as we love and serve one another in the Church, we reveal the invisible God.

> *And we all, with unveiled face, beholding the glory of the Lord, are being transformed into the same image from one degree of glory to another. For this comes from the Lord who is the Spirit.* (2 Corinthians 3:18)
>
> *"... By this all people will know that you are My disciples, if you have love for one another."* (John 13:35)

Of course, this does not mean we express His infinity, but we express His character, His nature.

What a privilege the Church now has – to reveal the invisible God! God has given us the privilege and responsibility of expressing the otherwise invisible God to the world.

Transformational Implications:

- Because God is invisible, we will avoid every form of idolatry.

> *You shall not make for yourself a carved image, or any likeness of anything that is in heaven above, or that is in the earth beneath, or that is in the water under the earth.* (Exodus 20:4)

- Because God is invisible, we will seek to know Him through His Son who reveals Himself to us by His indwelling Spirit.

> *For God, who said, "Let light shine out of darkness," has shone in our hearts to give the light of the knowledge of the glory of God in the face of Jesus Christ.* (2 Corinthians 4:6)

- Because God is invisible, we will seek to express His life through our lives and relationships so that others can "see God" in us.

> *No one has ever seen God; if we love one another, God abides in us and His love is perfected in us.* (1 John 4:12)

God Is Constant

All created things continually change – for better or for worse. Sometimes that change brings blessing and sometimes loss or pain. But because God is infinite and uncreated, He cannot change. He is outside of the world of change. He is perfect and complete, and He has always been so, and He will always be so.

> *Of old You laid the foundation of the earth, and the heavens are the work of Your hands. They will perish, but You will remain; they will all wear out like a garment. You will change them like a robe, and they will pass away, but You are the same, and Your years have no end.* (Psalm 102:25-27)

The psalmist makes a profound contrast between the created world, which is continually changing, and God who stays the same. He never changes.

> *And, "You, Lord, laid the foundation of the earth in the beginning, and the heavens are the work of Your hands; they will perish, but You remain; they will all wear out like a garment, like a robe You will roll them up, like a garment they will be changed. But You are the same, and Your years will have no end."* (Hebrews 1:10-12)
>
> *Jesus Christ is the same yesterday and today and forever.* (Hebrews 13:8)
>
> *Every good gift and every perfect gift is from above, coming down from the Father of lights, with whom there is no variation or shadow due to change.* (James 1:17)

However, to say that God is unchanging, does not mean that He is detached and passive. He is continually active in the world – in both major things and minor:

> *The Lord makes poor and makes rich; He brings low and He exalts. He raises up the poor from the dust; He lifts the needy from the ash heap to make them sit with princes and inherit a seat of honor. For the pillars of the earth are the Lord's, and on them He has set the world.* (1 Samuel 2:7–8)
>
> *... He makes His sun rise on the evil and on the good, and sends rain on the just and on the unjust.* (Matthew 5:45)
>
> *Are not two sparrows sold for a penny? And not one of them will fall to the ground apart from your Father.* (Matthew 10:29)

God is active in both judgment and redemption.

> *See now that I, even I, am He, and there is no god beside Me; I kill and I make alive; I wound and I heal; and there is none that can deliver out of My hand. For I lift up My hand to heaven and swear, As I live forever, if I sharpen My flashing sword and My hand takes hold on judgment, I will take vengeance on My adversaries and will repay those who hate Me.* (Deuteronomy 32:39-41)

When man sins, God judges him for his sin. And when men turn from their sin, He forgives them.

> *If My people who are called by My Name humble themselves, and pray and seek My face and turn from their wicked ways, then I will hear from heaven and will forgive their sin and heal their land.* (2 Chronicles 7:14)
>
> *If at any time I declare concerning a nation or a kingdom, that I will pluck up and break down and destroy it, and if that nation, concerning which I have spoken, turns from its evil, I will relent of the disaster that I intended to do to it. And if at any time I declare concerning a nation or a kingdom that I will build and plant it, and if it does evil in My sight, not listening to My voice, then I will relent of the good that I had intended to do to it.* (Jeremiah 18:7-10)

Therefore, as men interact with God, His responses to them will change. This may look like God changes. However, this does not indicate a change on God's part, but simply the expression of a different aspect of His eternal, unchanging Being.

For example, in the Book of Jonah, God declared that He fully intended to destroy the wicked city Nineveh in forty days (Jonah 3:4). But when the people of Nineveh repented (Jonah 3:5-9), God then "relented of the disaster that He had said He would do to them, and He did not do it" (Jonah 3:10). This does not represent a change in God's Being or character, but it was simply an expression of His mercy when they repented.

Just as God is holy and punishes sin, God is also merciful and forgives sin upon repentance. Both are unchanging characteristics of God. Just as His holiness never changes, so His mercy never changes either. The very reason God responds is because His nature is unchanging.

This means we can approach God with great certainty. Because He never changes, we know He will judge sin eventually. And because He never changes, when we repent and turn from our sin, we know He will forgive us.

Thus, while God is active and personal as He interacts with men, His eternal Being and nature never change.

If God did change, that would be awful! Perhaps He might change His mind about saving us. Perhaps He might bless sin and condemn righteousness. If God did change, how could we trust Him for anything?

But, since God does not change, His love and His promises remain certain – forever! We can trust Him. He will not change His mind. What He has said He will do.

> *For I the Lord do not change; therefore you, O children of Jacob, are not consumed. (Malachi 3:6)*

In Malachi 3, we see that God's mercy toward His people flows from His unchanging faithfulness to His own covenant of love. Because God does not change, His love is upon us forever. And because God never changes His promises to us, we can trust Him for everything with absolute certainty. He will not change His mind.

Transformational Implications:

- Because God never changes, His promises are secure. We can fully trust His Word.

  > *God is not man, that He should lie, or a son of man, that He should change His mind. Has He said, and will He not do it? Or has He spoken, and will He not fulfill it?* (Numbers 23:19)

  Even though we live in a world that is constantly changing and we are disappointed when we trust in men who say one thing but then do another, God never changes. Therefore, we can fully trust Him. The unchanging nature of God is the foundation of our faith.

- Because God does not change, we can come boldly to Him for the help we need while living in this ever-changing world.

  > *Not one word of all the good promises that the LORD had made to the house of Israel had failed; all came to pass. (Joshua 21:45)*

  This is God's promise to us and it gives us great boldness, strength and faith. Not one word of all the good promises that God has made to us will fail. All will come to pass. We can trust Him for everything because He is unchanging.

God Is Infinite

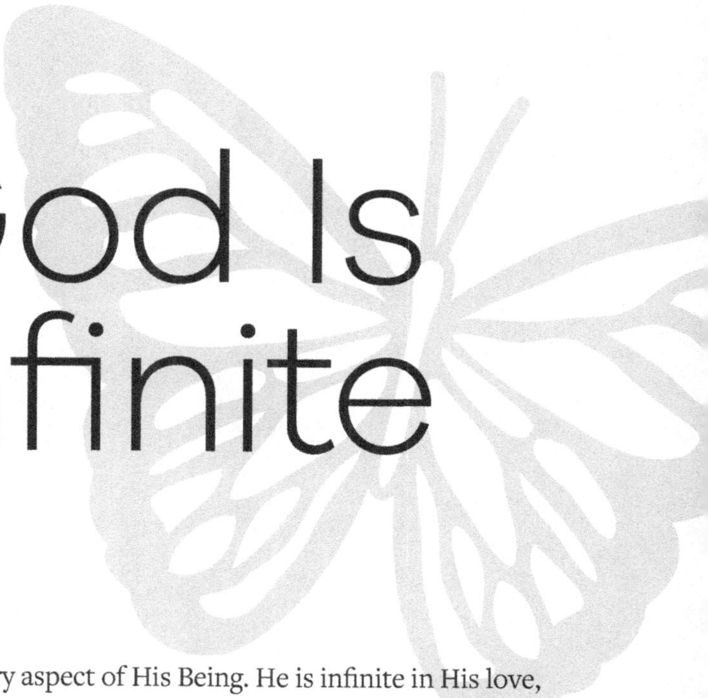

God is infinite in every aspect of His Being. He is infinite in His love, holiness and glory. In particular, He is infinite in His Presence, His knowledge and His power.

God Is Everywhere

As Spirit, God is infinite in His Presence, or "omnipresent."

> *But will God indeed dwell on the earth? Behold, heaven and the highest heaven cannot contain You; how much less this house that I have built!* (1 Kings 8:27)
>
> *Thus says the Lord: "Heaven is My throne, and the earth is My footstool; what is the house that you would build for Me, and what is the place of My rest?"* (Isaiah 66:1)

God's omnipresence does not merely mean that He is very big in size and so happens to be everywhere by virtue of that huge size. Just as God exists outside of time, He exists outside of the created world. Thus, God does not have size or spatial dimensions and is fully present at every point of space in both the physical and spiritual realms with His whole Being.

> *Where shall I go from Your Spirit? Or where shall I flee from Your Presence? If I ascend to heaven, You are there! If I make my bed in Sheol, You are there! If I take the wings of the morning and dwell in the uttermost parts of the sea, even there Your hand shall lead me, and Your right hand shall hold me.* (Psalm 139:7-10)

The psalmist wrote that there is nowhere we can go where God is not. He does not even have to turn His head from one thing to look at another! He simply is everywhere. Wherever we are, God is already there, and His love is there. Wherever we are, God will take us by the hand and lead us. This is the love and caring of God toward us. Whether we are running toward God in our lives or even trying to run away from Him, His hand is holding us. He never lets us go. We should not be intimidated by the infinite Presence of God – instead this is a source of great comfort and hope for us.

All of God is always fully with us. All of His love, all of His wisdom, all of His grace is with us. He is with us wherever we are. If we are doing well, He is with us. If we are doing badly, He is just as much with us. If we are in the church meeting worshiping God, He is with us. If we are at home washing the dishes after dinner, He is with us. If we are at work sweeping the floor, He is with us. All of God is always fully with us.

Since God is outside of the spatial world, He does not have to travel to get from one place to another. This was one of the taunts Elijah hurled at the prophets of Baal when their false god failed to answer:

> *And at noon Elijah mocked them, saying, "Cry aloud, for he is a god. Either he is musing, or he is relieving himself, or he is on a journey, or perhaps he is asleep and must be awakened."* (1 Kings 18:27)

The true God does not have this limitation. He is fully present all the time everywhere. He is fully present in the depths of the ocean and in the farthest reaches of outer space. Amazingly, God is fully present and fully engaged with every one of the billions of people alive on the earth today. He is with us, in every part of our lives!

> *Can a man hide himself in secret places so that I cannot see him? declares the Lord. Do I not fill heaven and earth? declares the Lord. (Jeremiah 23:24)*

At the same time, God acts differently in different places. He judges the wicked over here while He blesses the righteous over there.

Amazingly, God simultaneously gives His total and undivided attention not just to one thing at a time but to everything and everyone everywhere in His universe. And because He is outside of time, He does that in the past, present and future – all in the same moment. This is the God who says, "I will hold you by the hand and lead you."

> *Are not two sparrows sold for a penny? And not one of them will fall to the ground apart from your Father. But even the hairs of your head are all numbered.* (Matthew 10:29-30)

If God is fully engaged in the death of a sparrow, how much more is His undivided attention and care upon us! The God who created the heavens is always with us. His care is always upon us.

We do not have to go anywhere special to find Him. His full attention is upon us – always!

Whether we are running away from Him or running toward Him, He is always with us, His entire undivided attention is upon us – to lead us, to care for us, to hold us by the hand. He does not watch us out of the corner of His eye because He is looking at something more important. His full attention is always upon us.

Sometimes, we wonder about the negative things God allows in our lives. We wonder if He is still with us. The reality is that He is always with us! He is fully aware of it all, and in His wisdom, He allows the negative things to happen. Just as God allows good things to happen, He also allows bad things to happen. In this way, we can find great comfort in knowing that God is always with us, and His wise purposes will always be accomplished in whatever He allows to happen. Moreover, when we look at Him we will always find His Presence to support and encourage us, whatever we are going through. He never lets us go! We can let go of all anxiety and rest in His Presence, in His love and care.

> *"... And behold, I am with you always, to the end of the age."* (Matthew 28:20)

Transformational Implications:

- Because God is everywhere, we will recognize His personal involvement and care everywhere.

  > *Are not two sparrows sold for a penny? And not one of them will fall to the ground apart from your Father. But even the hairs of your head are all numbered. (Matthew 10:29-30; see also Matthew 6:25-34)*

God Is All-Knowing

God is infinite in knowledge, or "omniscient." There are many direct statements of this in the Scripture:

> *Do you know the balancings of the clouds, the wondrous works of Him who is perfect in knowledge?* (Job 37:16)
>
> *Great is our Lord, and abundant in power; His understanding is beyond measure.* (Psalm 147:5)
>
> *Have you not known? Have you not heard? The Lord is the everlasting God, the Creator of the ends of the earth. He does not faint or grow weary; His understanding is unsearchable.* (Isaiah 40:28)
>
> *Oh, the depth of the riches and wisdom and knowledge of God! How unsearchable are His judgments and how inscrutable His ways!* (Romans 11:33)

God's knowledge is "perfect," "beyond measure," "unsearchable" – it is infinite.

> *... God is greater than our heart, and He knows everything.* (1 John 3:20; *see also* Proverbs 15:11)

In 1 John 3, John makes a dramatic contrast between our own knowledge of ourselves and His knowledge of us. We tend to deceive ourselves and hide from the truth (Jeremiah 17:9). Those who follow the popular axiom, "Follow your heart," will inevitably fall into the ditch!

> *Whoever trusts in his own heart is a fool, but he who walks in wisdom will be delivered.* (Proverbs 28:26, Hebrew)

But God is greater than our hearts and He is not deceived. Consequently, we must look at Him, surrender to Him and depend on Him – only then can we know things as they really are. We must pray with the psalmist:

> *Search me, O God, and know my heart! Try me and know my thoughts! And see if there be any grievous way in me, and lead me in the way everlasting!* (Psalm 139:23-24)

Moreover, we must be transparent with God. Why try to fool Him? Sometimes Christians are worried about telling God what is really going on in their hearts and lives. They do not dare to say certain things to God; they are afraid of upsetting or disappointing Him – as if God does not already know it all!

It is not for His benefit that we should be honest with God; it is for our benefit. We need to face reality. To do this we need His help. He knows all things and He is greater than our hearts. We need His help to see things clearly.

God's infinite knowledge is seen in the fact that He fully knows Himself! Only infinite God could fully know infinite God.

> *... these things God has revealed to us through the Spirit. For the Spirit searches everything, even the depths of God. For who knows a person's thoughts except the spirit of that person, which is in him? So also no one comprehends the thoughts of God except the Spirit of God.* (1 Corinthians 2:10-11)

Again, this is why we are so utterly dependent on Him and what He reveals to us. If we are left to our own learning and wisdom, we will have no hope!

Because His knowledge is infinite, unlike us, God never learns anything, and He never forgets anything. All of His knowledge is always fully present in His mind.

> *And no creature is hidden from His sight, but all are naked and exposed to the eyes of Him to whom we must give account.* (Hebrews 4:13)

He knows everything about us – every thought, every motive, every secret of our hearts. God knows it all. Moreover, we must give an account to this God who knows it all. This gives us a healthy fear of God.

> *"I the Lord search the heart and test the mind, to give every man according to his ways, according to the fruit of his deeds."* (Jeremiah 17:10)

God knows every detail of our lives. Nothing surprises Him and there is nothing that escapes Him.

> *O Lord, You have searched me and known me! You know when I sit down and when I rise up; You discern my thoughts from afar. You search out my path and my lying down and are acquainted with all my ways. Even before a word is on my tongue, behold, O Lord, You know it altogether.* (Psalm 139:1-4)

We can rest in God's infinite knowledge. We do not have to figure everything out, or remember everything, or understand what happened in the past, or anticipate everything that may or may not happen in the future. God already knows it all! We can depend on Him.

> *And we know that for those who love God all things work together for good, for those who are called according to His purpose.* (Romans 8:28)

Jesus told us to not worry about tomorrow. God holds all of it in His hands. We do not know what is going to happen, but He does. So, we trust Him. We depend on Him regarding the past, the present, and the future, because He knows everything.

Transformational Implications:

- Because God is all-knowing, we will recognize that we need His help to truly know ourselves, our motives and our hearts.

  > *... God is greater than our heart, and He knows everything.* (1 John 3:20)

- Because God is all-knowing, we will not try to hide anything from Him. We will be transparent, opening the deep places in our hearts and lives to Him.

  > *O Lord, You have searched me and known me! You know when I sit down and when I rise up; You discern my thoughts from afar. You search out my path and my lying down and are acquainted with all my ways. Even before a word is on my tongue, behold, O Lord, You know it altogether.* (Psalm 139:1-4)

- Because God is all-knowing, we will have a healthy fear of God. One day we will give an account for our lives to the One from whom nothing is hidden.

  > *"I the Lord search the heart and test the mind, to give every man according to his ways, according to the fruit of his deeds."* (Jeremiah 17:10)

- Because God is all-knowing, we will rest in His infinite knowledge and trust His leading – not try to figure everything out, or remember everything, or understand what happened in the past, or anticipate everything that may or may not happen in the future. We will depend on the God who knows it all!

> *And we know that for those who love God all things work together for good, for those who are called according to His purpose.* (Romans 8:28)

God Is All-Powerful

God is infinite in power, or "omnipotent." Isaiah presents some beautiful, poetic expressions of God's omnipotence.

> *Who has measured the waters in the hollow of His hand and marked off the heavens with a span, enclosed the dust of the earth in a measure and weighed the mountains in scales and the hills in a balance?* (Isaiah 40:12)

God's omnipotence does not merely mean that He is very big in power or the most powerful Person around. God is Spirit. He is outside the created realm and not subject to its limitations. Thus, God's omnipotence means that there is nothing within the created world that He cannot do.

Moreover, it takes Him no more energy to do something small or great. It takes God no more effort to create the entire universe than to guide a single drop of rain as it falls to the earth. His power is infinite – not merely very big. He is outside the limitations of the physical world. It does not make any difference to Him whether He saves "by many or by few" (1 Samuel 14:6).

God does not have to exercise or eat well to keep His strength up. Neither does He need to rest between doing big things. We, of course, have to rest and eat so we can function, but God is infinite in power. He never grows weary:

> *Have you not known? Have you not heard? The Lord is the everlasting God, the Creator of the ends of the earth. He does not faint or grow weary; His understanding is unsearchable.* (Isaiah 40:28)

He does not have to choose between doing certain things because He only has enough energy for one of them. His power is infinite. There is nothing that is impossible for Him to do.

> *Is anything too hard for the Lord? ...* (Genesis 18:14)

In Genesis 18, God spoke these words to Abraham about having a son in his old age – he was about 100 (Romans 4:19)! It was impossible for man but not too hard for God.

To Mary, the young virgin woman, God also promised a child and she responded with faith:

> *"For nothing will be impossible with God."* (Luke 1:37)

In Job, Chapters 38 to 41, God gave great displays of His wisdom and power to Job, to which he responded:

> *I know that You can do all things, and that no purpose of Yours can be thwarted.* (Job 42:2)

Job realized that he needed to trust the God who is infinite in power instead of questioning why He allowed him to suffer.

There are other beautiful statements of God's omnipotence in the Scriptures:

> *Ah, Lord God! It is You who have made the heavens and the earth by Your great power and by Your outstretched arm! Nothing is too hard for You.* (Jeremiah 32:17)
>
> *But Jesus looked at them and said, "With man this is impossible, but with God all things are possible."* (Matthew 19:26)

One of God's names expresses His infinite power.

> *When Abram was ninety-nine years old the Lord appeared to Abram and said to him, "I am God Almighty; walk before Me, and be blameless ..." (Genesis 17:1)*

The Hebrew for "God Almighty" is *El-Shaddai* (יַּדַשׁ־לֵא) and it means that God has absolute power. He is the "All-mighty" One.

God possesses the fullness of His infinite power at all times. Amazingly, God does not have to choose between helping one or helping another because He only has enough energy to help one of us. All of His infinite power is fully available, all the time, everywhere. There are no exceptions.

He is the infinite God. All of God is everywhere, at the same time – infinite in knowledge and infinite in power! And this is the God who asks us to trust Him with our lives.

It is important to clarify that God is able to do whatever He chooses to do, and He will only choose to do what is consistent with His own perfect nature. Therefore, His infinite power will not be expressed in random, arbitrary or sinful ways. Instead, His infinite power is always expressed in harmony with His infinite wisdom, holiness and goodness. This is why God cannot lie (Titus 1:2), deny Himself (2 Timothy 2:13), or do evil (James 1:13) – these are things that God cannot do.

The gods of the pagans are not like this. They are moved by their moods. One day they do one thing; another day they do something else, according to their arbitrary feelings. But the true God who is infinite in power is the God who is infinite in wisdom, infinite in holiness, infinite in goodness, infinite in love.

So, we can trust Him. We can trust Him with our lives. We can trust Him with our churches, with our families, with our future. He has committed His infinite power to keep us.

We have great hope because of God's infinite power. The God on whom we depend for everything has committed the full measure of His unlimited ability to keep us!

> *... who by God's power are being guarded through faith for a salvation ready to be revealed in the last time.* (1 Peter 1:5)

On the Last Day, He will raise us up from the dead by His power.

> *And God raised the Lord and will also raise us up by His power.* (1 Corinthians 6:14)

Sometimes Christians worry about how God will be able to raise up the dead; for example, if a believer was cremated or buried at sea. But God will do it by His power – there is nothing too hard for Him!

In the meantime, during this life, God is able to make us thrive in every circumstance.

> *And God is able to make all grace abound to you, so that having all sufficiency in all things at all times, you may abound in every good work.* (2 Corinthians 9:8)

God is able to do this because He is infinite in power.

Moreover, we can preach the Gospel knowing that no one is beyond hope. God's infinite power will save everyone who comes to Him.

> *For I am not ashamed of the Gospel, for it is the power of God for salvation to everyone who believes, to the Jew first and also to the Greek.* (Romans 1:16)

When we share the Gospel with others, the infinite power of God stands behind us! When someone believes in Jesus, God will save him – no matter what he has done.

> *... He is able to save to the uttermost those who draw near to God through Him, since He always lives to make intercession for them.* (Hebrews 7:25)

Moreover, we should not give up on ourselves! Hebrews 7:25 is a promise to each of us. No matter how weak and incompetent we think we are, and no matter how many times we have failed, let us continue to draw near to God, trusting in His power to transform us into His own likeness.

Finally, God's infinite power should motivate us to ask and to expect great things from Him!

> *What then shall we say to these things? If God is for us, who can be against us?* (Romans 8:31)
>
> *Now to Him who is able to do far more abundantly than all that we ask or think, according to the power at work within us ...* (Ephesians 3:20)

God is able to do far more than anything we ask or could even imagine. His infinite power is with us. We should trust Him and be bold. Let us expect God to do great things, and not limit Him by our fear or unbelief. The God we serve is infinite in power.

The God of infinite power is in us and He is for us! Let us be bold and expect Him to do the impossible!

<u>Transformational Implications:</u>

- Because God is infinite in power, we will trust Him with our lives, with our churches, with our families and with our future.

  > *... who by God's power are being guarded through faith for a salvation ready to be revealed in the last time.* (1 Peter 1:5)

- Because God is all-powerful, we should never give up on anyone, including ourselves. He is able to save and change everyone, no matter how hopeless their situation appears.

> *... He is able to save to the uttermost those who draw near to God through Him, since He always lives to make intercession for them.* (Hebrews 7:25)

- Because God is all-powerful, we will not limit Him. Instead, we will expectantly ask Him to do great things!

> *What then shall we say to these things? If God is for us, who can be against us?* (Romans 8:31)
>
> *Now to Him who is able to do far more abundantly than all that we ask or think, according to the power at work within us ...* (Ephesians 3:20)

The infinite power of God is for us! Nothing can overcome us because God is for us!

God Is Love

God Is Love

If God were infinite in Presence, knowledge and power, but were not Love, we would be in serious trouble.

Imagine a god who is infinite in power, who can do anything he wants; a god who is infinite in knowledge, who knows everything about our lives and every wrong thought we have ever had; a god who is infinite in presence, so we cannot escape him. Then imagine that this god is *not* love; instead, he is capricious and arbitrary. Such a god would be terrifying!

However, the true God's love is as infinite as He is. Love is His very nature – His very Being.

> *Anyone who does not love does not know God, because God is love. (1 John 4:8)*

Please notice that John does not say that God *has* love or that God is *loving*, but that God *is* love. All of His infinite Being is love.

For eternity, God is love. Before the creation of the world, in the triune Being of God, the Father perfectly loved the Son, who perfectly loved the Father. The Holy Spirit perfectly loved the Father and the Son and was loved by them.

> *Father ... You loved Me before the foundation of the world. (John 17:24)*

Moreover, love is not merely a word or an emotional feeling. True love is an action, an action of giving, an action of self-giving. Thus, the Father loved and gave Himself fully to the Son who, in turn, gave Himself fully to the Father, and to the Holy Spirit likewise.

Moreover, God then created man in His own image so that man could receive His self-giving love and give himself back to God. Man went his own way and sinned and his relationship with God was broken, but God's self-giving love was still expressed toward us. God's supreme expression of love was in Jesus giving Himself on the Cross.

> *For God so loved the world, that He gave His only Son, that whoever believes in Him should not perish but have eternal life.* (John 3:16)
>
> *... but God shows His love for us in that while we were still sinners, Christ died for us.* (Romans 5:8)

Even when we hated Him and were His enemies, God loved us with an infinite love and gave Himself for us.

> *By this we know love, that He laid down His life for us ...* (1 John 3:16)
>
> *In this is love, not that we have loved God but that He loved us and sent His Son to be the propitiation for our sins.* (1 John 4:10)

When God gave His Son for us, He gave us a far greater treasure than all the riches of the universe put together. He gave us Himself!

Amazingly, in His love, God not only freely loved us, but He sought after us to give us His love – and He did this while we were still sinners!

> *"What man of you, having a hundred sheep, if he has lost one of them, does not leave the ninety-nine in the open country, and go after the one that is lost, until he finds it? And when he has found it, he lays it on his shoulders, rejoicing. And when he comes home, he calls together his friends and his neighbors, saying to them, 'Rejoice with me, for I have found my sheep that was lost.' Just so, I tell you, there will be more joy in heaven over one sinner who repents*

> *than over ninety-nine righteous persons who need no repentance ..."* (Luke 15:4-7)

This is the God we serve: the God who loved us and died for us even when we were His enemies and then sought us out to give us the great salvation He purchased for us!

Having now received His love, we are to love God with the same self-giving love, holding nothing back from Him – giving ourselves fully to the God who is love.

> *We love because He first loved us.* (1 John 4:19)

For all eternity we will explore the depths of the riches of the love of God. We will never get bored with this. We will look at God in His fullness, we will experience His beauty, His glory, His love!

Moreover, now in this life, from our union with the God who is infinite love, we will also have love for others.

> *Beloved, let us love one another, for love is from God, and whoever loves has been born of God and knows God. Anyone who does not love does not know God, because God is love. In this the love of God was made manifest among us, that God sent His only Son into the world, so that we might live through Him. In this is love, not that we have loved God but that He loved us and sent His Son to be the propitiation for our sins. Beloved, if God so loved us, we also ought to love one another. No one has ever seen God; if we love one another, God abides in us and His love is perfected in us.* (1 John 4:7-12)

These are the two great commandments. They are both commandments of love!

> *And He said to him, "You shall love the Lord your God with all your heart and with all your soul and with all your mind. This is the great and first commandment. And a second is like it: You shall love your neighbor as yourself. On these two commandments depend all the Law and the Prophets."* (Matthew 22:37-40)

Transformational Implications:

- Because God is love, we will embrace His incredible invitation to participate in the eternal self-giving love of the triune God. Because we are made in His image, we can receive His infinite, glorious, magnificent, self-giving love.

  And, again because we are in His image, we can love Him back, just as He gives Himself to us – we can give ourselves back to Him.

  > *... that which we have seen and heard we proclaim also to you, so that you too may have fellowship with us; and indeed our fellowship is with the Father and with His Son Jesus Christ.* (1 John 1:3)

- Out of this experience of His love, we will then seek to love others with the same self-giving love.

  > *By this we know love, that He laid down His life for us, and we ought to lay down our lives for the brothers.* (1 John 3:16)

God Is Personal

Some people have a philosophical view of God that understands Him as a Creator who set the universe in motion and established the laws that would govern what happens in the world, and then stepped back and is no longer actively engaged with His creation – like a watchmaker who wound up a watch and then let it run under its own power without any further personal involvement from him.

Biblically, however, the infinite and almighty God is personally, deeply and passionately involved with His creation.

The Bible teaches that God is both infinite and personal. Because He is infinite, He has no limitations of any kind, and He is immeasurably greater than the sum total of everything in creation. Yet, because He is also personal, He interacts with us in a personal and intimate way, and we relate to Him in an intimate way.

We are welcome to approach Him, pray to Him, worship Him, talk to Him, listen to Him, know Him! We can tell Him of all our little problems and concerns, and He listens to it all. Then He speaks to us – about great things and small things. He loves us, cares for us, rejoices in us. We can know Him as our closest Friend.

Significantly, God has a Name (Exodus 3:14) – He is not merely an abstract, nameless force. He is personal and the Scriptures speak of Him in very personal ways.

He is our Father (Matthew 6:9), our Shepherd (John 10:11), our Helper (John 14:16), our Refuge (Psalm 46:1), our Protector (Psalm

91), our Savior (2 Timothy 1:10). The infinite God who created the heavens calls us His "friends" – we are the friends of God!

> *No longer do I call you servants, for the servant does not know what his master is doing; but I have called you friends, for all that I have heard from My Father I have made known to you.* (John 15:15)

God is so personal He makes His home with us. We are His dwelling place.

> *Jesus answered him, "If anyone loves Me, he will keep My Word, and My Father will love him, and We will come to him and make Our home with him."* (John 14:23)
>
> *In Him you also are being built together into a dwelling place for God by the Spirit.* (Ephesians 2:22)

There are many examples in the Scripture of God's deep and personal concern for man.

> *If you then, who are evil, know how to give good gifts to your children, how much more will your Father who is in heaven give good things to those who ask Him!* (Matthew 7:11)

In Matthew 7:11, Jesus gives both a comparison and a contrast. First, just as we love to give good gifts to our children and grandchildren, so does God. There is such gentleness and intimacy in this description. But then the contrast: we know how much we love to give good things to our children, but God loves to do this far more! He does this with far more affection and joy than we do.

We also see God's deep affection and care for His people in the fact that He takes attacks against them very personally:

> *Then the Lord said, "I have surely seen the affliction of My people who are in Egypt and have heard their cry because of their taskmasters. I know their sufferings, and I have come down to deliver them out of the hand of the Egyptians and to bring them up out of that land*

> *to a good and broad land, a land flowing with milk and honey ... And now, behold, the cry of the people of Israel has come to Me, and I have also seen the oppression with which the Egyptians oppress them ..."* (Exodus 3:7-9)
>
> *He found him in a desert land, and in the howling waste of the wilderness; He encircled him, He cared for him, He kept him as the apple of His eye.* (Deuteronomy 32:10)
>
> *In all their affliction He was afflicted, and the Angel of His Presence saved them; in His love and in His pity He redeemed them; He lifted them up and carried them all the days of old.* (Isaiah 63:9)
>
> *For thus said the Lord of hosts, after His glory sent me to the nations who plundered you, for he who touches you touches the apple of His eye:* (Zechariah 2:8)
>
> *And the King will answer them, "Truly, I say to you, as you did it to one of the least of these My brothers, you did it to Me."* (Matthew 25:40)
>
> *And falling to the ground, he heard a Voice saying to him, "Saul, Saul, why are you persecuting Me?"* (Acts 9:4)

God takes it all so personally. He is not somewhere watching us at a distance, vaguely concerned. He is personally, deeply, and passionately engaged.

Even toward the wicked and disobedient, God is personally and deeply moved:

> *Oh, that My people would listen to Me, that Israel would walk in My ways!* (Psalm 81:13)
>
> *... but, though He cause grief, He will have compassion according to the abundance of His steadfast love; for He does not afflict from His heart or grieve the children of men.* (Lamentations 3:32-33)

> *Say to them, "As I live," declares the Lord God, "I have no pleasure in the death of the wicked, but that the wicked turn from his way and live; turn back, turn back from your evil ways, for why will you die, O house of Israel?"* (Ezekiel 33:11)
>
> *"How can I give you up, O Ephraim? How can I hand you over, O Israel? How can I make you like Admah[4]? How can I treat you like Zeboiim? My heart recoils within Me; My compassion grows warm and tender."* (Hosea 11:8)
>
> *When He saw the crowds, He had compassion for them, because they were harassed and helpless, like sheep without a shepherd.* (Matthew 9:36)
>
> *"O Jerusalem, Jerusalem, the city that kills the prophets and stones those who are sent to it! How often would I have gathered your children together as a hen gathers her brood under her wings, and you were not willing!"* (Matthew 23:37)
>
> *And when He drew near and saw the city, He wept over it, saying, "Would that you, even you, had known on this day the things that make for peace! But now they are hidden from your eyes. For the days will come upon you, when your enemies will set up a barricade around you and surround you and hem you in on every side and tear you down to the ground, you and your children within you. And they will not leave one stone upon another in you, because you did not know the time of your visitation."* (Luke 19:41-44)

We see the heart of God in all these passages. He is deeply moved by the condition of the lost. Jesus wept over rebellious Jerusalem.

For us, also, the destruction of the wicked should not be merely a cold, theoretical doctrine. We should be deeply moved by it as the Old Testament prophets were. They did not simply point their

---

4 Admah and Zeboiim were cities that were totally destroyed along with Sodom and Gomorrah (Deuteronomy 29:23).

accusing finger at the rebellious and declare judgment on them. The prophets were grieved and compassionate towards them.

> *Therefore I said: "Look away from me; let me weep bitter tears; do not labor to comfort me concerning the destruction of the daughter of my people." (Isaiah 22:4)*

After pronouncing judgment, Isaiah says this about himself, "Don't look at me. Let me weep bitter tears. Don't try to comfort me. My heart is too deeply broken. I cannot be comforted."

Jeremiah expresses this same deep grief toward those who were being judged by God. He is broken by this. This is true prophetic ministry – Jeremiah is united with God in His grief and anguish, and compassion for the lost.

> *My anguish, my anguish! I writhe in pain! Oh the walls of my heart! My heart is beating wildly; I cannot keep silent, for I hear the sound of the trumpet, the alarm of war. (Jeremiah 4:19)*
>
> *Oh that my head were waters, and my eyes a fountain of tears, that I might weep day and night for the slain of the daughter of my people! (Jeremiah 9:1)*
>
> *But if you will not listen, my soul will weep in secret for your pride; my eyes will weep bitterly and run down with tears, because the Lord's flock has been taken captive. (Jeremiah 13:17)*

This is where true revivals are born – in this union with Christ, in this union with His compassionate and grieved heart. In Isaiah and Jeremiah and now in us, this union with the heart of God becomes a deep prayer of intercession. This is a deep experience of union with Christ, where we are borne along by His pain, by His sorrow and by His compassion for the lost. This becomes a prayer of deep travail, a deep intercession for the lost from which revivals are born.

Furthermore, in our concern for the lost, we should be considerate to everyone.

> *And the Lord's servant must not be quarrelsome but kind to everyone, able to teach, patiently enduring evil, correcting his opponents with gentleness. God may perhaps grant them repentance leading to a knowledge of the truth, and they may come to their senses and escape from the snare of the devil, after being captured by him to do his will.* (2 Timothy 2:24-26)

Paul speaks here to Timothy about those who are opposing the Gospel, and he says to be kind to them. We must be kind to everyone, expressing the personal kindness of God to man.

Moreover, because God is personal, He must not be treated as an object or force to be used or manipulated. Often Christians see God as simply something to be used to solve our problems and meet our needs. Such an attitude belongs in the realm of magic or technology, and not in our relationship with the living God who has called us to be His friends!

> *... whoever would draw near to God must believe that He exists and that He rewards those who seek Him.* (Hebrews 11:6)

God is a rewarder of those who seek *Him*, not merely those who seek things from Him. He wants to give us Himself! Then, as we love Him and walk with Him, He delights to bless us.

The God who is infinite in Presence, knowledge and power, the God who is the Lord of history, raising up one empire and putting down another, is, at the same time, deeply personal and intimate with His children, loving to give us good things. This is the true God.

Apart from the true revelation of God that is found in the Bible, there is no religion that has a God who is both infinite and personal. The living God is not only the Sovereign Lord who rules all nations and all history, He is also kind to everyone. Both are brought together here:

> *Your Kingdom is an everlasting Kingdom, and Your dominion endures throughout all generations. The Lord is faithful in all His words and kind in all His works.* (Psalm 145:13)

This is the God we serve. He is passionately concerned about our lives. He cares deeply for us. He wants to relate intimately to us. He wants us to know Him! Moreover, He wants nothing but good for us.

Transformational Implications:

- Because God is personal, we can have a relationship with Him. We can be friends with Him. We can draw near to Him, knowing that He knows us intimately, cares very deeply for us and wants us to intimately know Him. What an extraordinary privilege we have!

  > *For we do not have a High Priest who is unable to sympathize with our weaknesses, but One who in every respect has been tempted as we are, yet without sin. Let us then with confidence draw near to the throne of grace, that we may receive mercy and find grace to help in time of need. (Hebrews 4:15-16)*

- Because God is personal, we will seek to express His personal care to those around us, especially to the lost.

  > *Walk in wisdom toward outsiders, making the best use of the time. Let your speech always be gracious, seasoned with salt, so that you may know how you ought to answer each person. (Colossians 4:5-6)*

- Because God is personal, He is to be treated personally. He must not be treated as an object or force to be used or manipulated.

  > *... whoever would draw near to God must believe that He exists and that He rewards those who seek Him. (Hebrews 11:6)*

God Is Good

All that God does is good because He is good.

> *For the Lord is good; His steadfast love endures forever, and His faithfulness to all generations.* (Psalm 100:5)
>
> *Give thanks to the Lord, for He is good, for His steadfast love endures forever.* (Psalm 136:1)

Many years ago, one of the leaders in my church became very sick, almost to the point of death. It was as if she did die and was in a place between life and death. There she experienced a profound sense of the goodness of God. She saw the great light of God. She felt the great love of God. In particular, she experienced the deep goodness of God toward her. When she came back, she said this to me, "I experienced the goodness of God toward me. In God, there was nothing but goodness!" That was her testimony: God is nothing but good toward us. He is the perfect, infinitely loving Heavenly Father. Our Heavenly Father.

We love our own children and grandchildren dearly. We can think of a time when there was the purest of love, of joy, of goodness in our heart toward our children and grandchildren. That is just a shadow of God's attitude toward us all the time! He is nothing but good toward us.

In His goodness, God is kind and generous to all:

> *Praise the Lord, all nations! Extol Him, all peoples! For great is His steadfast love toward us, and the faithfulness of the Lord endures forever. Praise the Lord!* (Psalm 117:1-2)
>
> *The Lord is good to all, and His mercy is over all that He has made.* (Psalm 145:9)
>
> *Yet He did not leave Himself without witness, for He did good by giving you rains from heaven and fruitful seasons, satisfying your hearts with food and gladness.* (Acts 14:17)

In Acts 14:17, Paul addresses the lost and says God is good to them. God is good to the lost!

Sometimes Christians wonder if they have been righteous enough to deserve God's goodness toward them. And they assume they have not been, so they live without a deep sense of His goodness. But God is good to all – freely. Even when He chastises us as our loving Heavenly Father, that is an expression of His goodness to us.

> *"For the Lord disciplines the one He loves, and chastises every son whom He receives."* (Hebrews 12:6)

God's goodness is seen throughout His creation:

> *From Your lofty abode You water the mountains; the earth is satisfied with the fruit of Your work. You cause the grass to grow for the livestock and plants for man to cultivate, that he may bring forth food from the earth and wine to gladden the heart of man, oil to make his face shine and bread to strengthen man's heart ... These all look to You, to give them their food in due season. When You give it to them, they gather it up; when You open Your hand, they are filled with good things.* (Psalm 104:13-15, 27-28)
>
> *Look at the birds of the air: they neither sow nor reap nor gather into barns, and yet your Heavenly Father feeds them. Are you not of more value than they?* (Matthew 6:26)

> *But if God so clothes the grass of the field, which today is alive and tomorrow is thrown into the oven, will He not much more clothe you, O you of little faith?* (Matthew 6:30)

If God is so good to His natural creation, how much more will He be good to us who are created in His image, and for whom Jesus gave His life?

> *Fear not, little flock, for it is your Father's good pleasure to give you the Kingdom.* (Luke 12:32)

Jesus said that God takes pleasure in being good to us!

Because we know that God is good, we can trust Him in suffering and difficult times.

> *For I know the plans I have for you, declares the Lord, plans for welfare and not for evil, to give you a future and a hope.* (Jeremiah 29:11)

Jeremiah was prophesying to Judah in a terrible time. They were being destroyed by Babylon for their sin. But even to them, God says, I am giving you "a future and a hope." That was God's promise to those who were deeply sinful and had rejected Him. If God promised His goodness to them, how much more to us who are in Christ?

This is why we should rejoice in His goodness toward us!

> *Let those who delight in My righteousness shout for joy and be glad and say evermore, "Great is the Lord, who delights in the welfare of His servant!"* (Psalm 35:27)

We should rejoice always (1 Thessalonians 5:16), not feeling sorry for ourselves when we are struggling. Instead, we should shout for joy at His goodness.

As our loving Heavenly Father, God continually provides for us in so many ways. Here are some practical examples of His goodness to us in our daily lives:

- God knows and cares about our needs. (Matthew 6:8, 32)
- He faithfully gives us our daily bread. (Matthew 6:11)
- He gives us everything we need as we seek first His Kingdom. (Matthew 6:33)
- He gives wisdom generously to all. (James 1:5)
- He chastises us when we need it. (Hebrews 12:5-11)
- He comforts us in our sufferings. (2 Corinthians 1:5)
- He teaches us. (John 16:13)
- He gives us strength. (Ephesians 3:16)
- He gives us peace. (John 14:27)
- He gives us security. (John 10:27-30)
- He gives us hope for the future. (2 Thessalonians 2:16)
- He meets all of our needs according to His riches in glory in Christ Jesus. (Philippians 4:19)

We are surrounded by the goodness of God. But this is not because we deserve it. It is because it is His nature. God is good.

In particular, God's mercy is His goodness expressed toward those who are in pain or distress of some kind:

> *Then David said to Gad, "I am in great distress. Let us fall into the hand of the Lord, for His mercy is great; but let me not fall into the hand of man."* (2 Samuel 24:14)
>
> *And as Jesus passed on from there, two blind men followed Him, crying aloud, "Have mercy on us, Son of David."* (Matthew 9:27)
>
> *Let us then with confidence draw near to the throne of grace, that we may receive mercy and find grace to help in time of need.* (Hebrews 4:16)

Profoundly, God is not only good toward His own family. He is also kind and generous to those who do not know Him.

> *... your Father who is in heaven ... makes His sun rise on the evil and on the good, and sends rain on the just and on the unjust.* (*Matthew 5:45*)

Since God is good to us, we will have the same love and care to others – especially for those who are needy – and we will express His extravagant generosity consistently.

> *Who is like the LORD our God, who is seated on high, who looks far down on the heavens and the earth? He raises the poor from the dust and lifts the needy from the ash heap, to make them sit with princes, with the princes of His people. He gives the barren woman a home, making her the joyous mother of children. Praise the LORD!* (*Psalm 113:5-9*)
>
> *And God is able to make all grace abound to you, so that having all sufficiency in all things at all times, you may abound in every good work.* (*2 Corinthians 9:8*)
>
> *Religion that is pure and undefiled before God the Father is this: to visit orphans and widows in their affliction, and to keep oneself unstained from the world.* (*James 1:27*)
>
> *If a brother or sister is poorly clothed and lacking in daily food, and one of you says to them, "Go in peace, be warmed and filled," without giving them the things needed for the body, what good is that?* (*James 2:15-16*)

And this is just the beginning. For eternity, God's goodness will be poured out upon those who love Him. If He has so much goodness toward us now during our lives on the earth, what will we experience in eternity – when God has taken all sin away and wiped every tear from our eyes? We will swim in the vast ocean of His goodness.

> *... For all things are yours, whether ... the world or life or death or the present or the future – all are yours, and you are Christ's, and Christ is God's.* (*1 Corinthians 3:21-23*)

> *... so that in the coming ages He might show the immeasurable riches of His grace in kindness toward us in Christ Jesus.* (*Ephesians 2:7*)

This is the God we serve![5]

Transformational Implications:

- Because God is good, we can trust Him in suffering and difficult times.

  > *For I know the plans I have for you, declares the LORD, plans for welfare and not for evil, to give you a future and a hope.* (*Jeremiah 29:11*)

- Because God is good, we will rejoice in His goodness toward us!

  > *Let those who delight in My righteousness shout for joy and be glad and say evermore, "Great is the LORD, who delights in the welfare of His servant!"* (*Psalm 35:27*)

- Because God is good, we will express His extravagant generosity consistently to others, especially to the needy.

  > *And God is able to make all grace abound to you, so that having all sufficiency in all things at all times, you may abound in every good work.* (*2 Corinthians 9:8*)

5 For more on the goodness and generosity of God, please see *Shaping a Culture of Generosity* by Malcolm Webber.

God Is Gracious

God is good and kind to everyone, whether or not they deserve it.[6] This is God's grace, His undeserved favor.

> *... the Most High ... is kind to the ungrateful and the evil.* (Luke 6:35)
>
> *In past generations He allowed all the nations to walk in their own ways. Yet He did not leave Himself without witness, for He did good by giving you rains from heaven and fruitful seasons, satisfying your hearts with food and gladness.* (Acts 14:16-17)

In particular, God's grace is spectacularly revealed in His amazing provision of salvation for those who deserved eternal death.

> *... for all have sinned and fall short of the glory of God, and are justified by His grace as a gift, through the redemption that is in Christ Jesus ...* (Romans 3:23-24)
>
> *... but God shows His love for us in that while we were still sinners, Christ died for us.* (Romans 5:8)

God would have been perfectly righteous in sending us all to eternal judgment; we deserved it. We were lovers of sin and haters of God, and yet Jesus died for us. There is no greater gift that God could have given us. We deserved eternal death and yet God gave the life of His Son to save us. That is undeserved goodness – the grace of God.

---

6 This does not mean that He saves everyone; He only saves those who come to Christ (John 3:3, 36).

What a tragedy it would be if someone understood the grace of God, agreeing with it as an abstract philosophical idea, but never acted on it and gave their life to the Lord Jesus and received His grace and eternal life.

Moreover, in His goodness, God is longsuffering toward those who deserve His judgment and refuse to come to Christ.

> *The Lord passed before him and proclaimed, "The Lord, the Lord, a God merciful and gracious, slow to anger, and abounding in steadfast love and faithfulness ..."* (Exodus 34:6)
>
> *The Lord is not slow to fulfill His promise as some count slowness, but is patient toward you, not wishing that any should perish, but that all should reach repentance.* (2 Peter 3:9)

God's desire is always that the lost will turn to Him and be saved. When God delays His wrath in His patience, that in itself is an expression of goodness. In His grace He gives people the opportunity to repent.

> *Or do you presume on the riches of His kindness and forbearance and patience, not knowing that God's kindness is meant to lead you to repentance?* (Romans 2:4)

As His children, those who have received God's goodness and grace must be careful to give the same goodness and grace to others – especially when they do not deserve it.

> *But love your enemies, and do good, and lend, expecting nothing in return, and your reward will be great, and you will be sons of the Most High, for He is kind to the ungrateful and the evil.* (Luke 6:35)

The way of the world is to destroy our enemies, but Jesus says to love them and do good to them – and then our reward will be great!

> *Be kind to one another, tenderhearted, forgiving one another, as God in Christ forgave you.* (Ephesians 4:32)

We must be like our Heavenly Father. He is good to those who do not deserve it, and we must do the same. It is easy to be good to people when they are good to us and kind to us, but by the grace of God, by His indwelling power, He will give us the ability to forgive and do good to those who do not deserve it – people who have treated us badly, people who have opposed us, people who have hurt us or those close to us, people who have misrepresented us, people who have stolen from us.

> *But I say to you, Love your enemies and pray for those who persecute you, so that you may be sons of your Father who is in heaven. For He makes His sun rise on the evil and on the good, and sends rain on the just and on the unjust. For if you love those who love you, what reward do you have? Do not even the tax collectors do the same? And if you greet only your brothers, what more are you doing than others? Do not even the Gentiles do the same? You therefore must be perfect, as your Heavenly Father is perfect.* (Matthew 5:44-48)

When we do this, then we understand the doctrine of the grace of God.

Transformational Implications:

- Because God is gracious, we will, with everlasting gratitude, receive His undeserved gift of forgiveness and life.

  > *Give thanks to the Lord, for He is good, for His steadfast love endures forever.* (Psalm 136:1)

- Because God is gracious, as His children who have received His grace, we will be careful to show the same grace to others – especially when they do not deserve it.

  > *But love your enemies, and do good, and lend, expecting nothing in return, and your reward will be great, and you will be sons of the Most High, for He is kind to the ungrateful and the evil.* (Luke 6:35)

God Is Beautiful

God Himself is the perfection of beauty.

> *For how great is His goodness, and how great His beauty! ...* (*Zechariah 9:17*)

He reigns on a glorious throne that is stunningly beautiful.

> *... and they saw the God of Israel. There was under His feet as it were a pavement of sapphire stone, like the very heaven for clearness.* (*Exodus 24:10*)
>
> *Out of Zion, the perfection of beauty, God shines forth.* (Psalm 50:2)
>
> *Splendor and majesty are before Him; strength and beauty are in His sanctuary.* (Psalm 96:6)
>
> *At once I was in the Spirit, and behold, a throne stood in heaven, with One seated on the throne. And He who sat there had the appearance of jasper and carnelian, and around the throne was a rainbow that had the appearance of an emerald ... and before the throne there was as it were a sea of glass, like crystal.* (Revelation 4:2-3, 6)

God Himself is the perfection of beauty, the ultimate beauty, and everything He has made expresses His beauty and His desire for beauty.

God could have created a world that was perfectly functional but bland and dull. But instead, He created an almost limitless variety of incredibly beautiful things.

In the heavens, God created an almost infinite number of stars and galaxies, breathtaking in beauty, all declaring His glory.

On the earth, God made the oceans, the mountains, the deserts, and the rivers. He created millions of species of insects, hundreds of thousands of species of flowers, tens of thousands of kinds of edible plants, and thousands of species of birds.

He did not have to make all these beautiful things, but He wanted His world to be beautiful because that is what He is like. When we look at the world, we should see the power and wisdom of God in its creation (Romans 1:20), but we should also see His beauty and worship Him.

When God looked at His creation in the beginning, He saw that "it was good" (Genesis 1:25). He did not only mean it was functional – that it works very well. More than that, it was also beautiful. God is a beautiful God and He loves beauty.

Then God created His most beautiful creature – mankind. He gave us the capacity to know Him and to love others. He created sound, music, color, shape. He gave us the senses of sight, hearing, touch, smell and taste. And He did all this to bless us!

God gave us the ability to appreciate the beauty that He created for us. He created all this beauty for us; He did not need it for Himself. He is already infinitely beautiful and infinitely satisfied with His own beauty. He created this beautiful world for us to enjoy.

He gave us the five senses so that we would be able to enjoy it: sight so that we can see His beauty, hearing so that we can hear the beautiful things He has created, taste so we can enjoy delicious food. God could have just given us manna and that would have nourished us physically. But thank God He did not. Instead, He gave us a vast number of foods that are not only good for us, but also taste good. He gave us the sense of smell so we can smell the flowers, and touch so we can feel softness, texture and warmth. This is who God is. He is a beautiful God and everything He created expresses His beauty.

> *... God, who richly provides us with everything to enjoy.* (1 Timothy 6:17)

Sometimes Christians feel bad about enjoying the beautiful things of this life in this world. But God tells us that He created these beautiful things so that we will enjoy them now.

Of course, God does not want us to set our hearts on those things and turn away from Him. But we should look at a beautiful sunset and say, "Jesus, You are awesome!" When we taste delicious food, we should say, "Thank You, Jesus!" When we look at the beauty of the colors of flowers we should say, "Lord, I love You!"

> *Do not love the world or the things in the world. If anyone loves the world, the love of the Father is not in him. For all that is in the world – the desires of the flesh and the desires of the eyes and pride of life – is not from the Father but is from the world. And the world is passing away along with its desires, but whoever does the will of God abides forever.* (1 John 2:15–17)

When John says, "do not love the world," he is not saying that we are forbidden from enjoying a flower. He is referring to the moral world that we are not to love: "the desires of the flesh and the desires of the eyes and pride of life." Those lusts are not of God. But when we look at the beautiful things that God has created with our hearts fully set on Him, worshiping Him, praising Him, thanking Him, giving Him glory, that is appropriate. God wants us to enjoy the beauty of the world He has created and worship Him.

When man sinned and fell, the created world became corrupted – its beauty was marred (Romans 8:20-21). Now it does not have the same beauty that it once had when God first created the world. Neither does it have the same beauty that the new heavens and earth will have (Isaiah 65:17; 2 Peter 3:12-13). Nevertheless, the current world still reflects God's beauty.

> *O Lord, our Lord, how majestic is Your Name in all the earth! You have set Your glory above the heavens ... When I look at Your heavens, the work of Your fingers, the moon and the stars, which You have set in place, what is man that You are mindful of him, and the son of man that You care for him? ... O Lord, our Lord, how majestic is Your Name in all the earth!* (Psalm 8:1, 3-4, 9)
>
> *The heavens declare the glory of God, and the sky above proclaims His handiwork.* (Psalm 19:1)

Please notice how the psalmist looks at the beauty of the heavens and then his heart worships God. The pagan looks at the beautiful heavens and worships the moon and the stars. That is idolatry and sin. But when we look at the beautiful things God has created, our hearts are lifted up to Him – we look at Him, we love Him, we worship Him.

In particular, God wants us to personally experience His own beauty.

> *You make known to me the path of life; in Your Presence there is fullness of joy; at Your right hand are pleasures forevermore.* (Psalm 16:11)

Psalm 16 is a Messianic psalm referring to Jesus' resurrection and ascension, but it also shows us what *we* have to look forward to after our resurrection: pleasures forevermore! In God's Presence there is eternal beauty and pleasure.

> *One thing have I asked of the Lord, that will I seek after: that I may dwell in the house of the Lord all the days of my life, to gaze upon the beauty of the Lord and to inquire in His temple.* (Psalm 27:4)

The truly spiritual person has a passion to be in the Presence of God so he can gaze upon the beauty of the Lord. God wants us to see His beauty, to love His beauty, to enjoy His beauty.

> *How precious is Your steadfast love, O God! The children of mankind take refuge in the shadow of Your wings. They feast on the abundance of Your house, and You give them drink from the river of Your delights. For with You is the fountain of life; in Your light do we see light.* (Psalm 36:7-9)

He wants us to delight in Him – truly to enjoy Him!

> *Delight yourself in the Lord, and He will give you the desires of your heart.* (Psalm 37:4)
>
> *Whom have I in heaven but You? And there is nothing on earth that I desire besides You.* (Psalm 73:25)

As we delight ourselves in God, we should also enjoy the beautiful things He has made. It is not sinful or worldly to do so. God created beautiful things for us!

Throughout God's words to Job, He repeatedly urges him to look at the beauty, wonder and amazing design of all the things that He in His wisdom has created (Job 38 – 41).

We should enjoy the beauty of God's creation: flowers, coral reefs, waterfalls, tiny insects, majestic trees, vast canyons, sunsets and sunrises, powerful storms and lightning displays, dew-covered cobwebs, the glorious palette of colors that is splashed over all of nature, and the wonder of the rainbows. All of this is given to us by God to point us to Him as the supremely beautiful Creator.

Since God Himself gave us all of this extraordinary beauty to point to His glory, we also should use beauty intentionally to honor Him and give Him glory.

> *The Lord said to Moses, "See, I have called by name Bezalel the son of Uri, son of Hur, of the tribe of Judah, and I have filled him with the Spirit of God, with ability and intelligence, with knowledge and all craftsmanship, to devise artistic designs, to work in gold, silver,*

> *and bronze, in cutting stones for setting, and in carving wood, to work in every craft."* (Exodus 31:1-5)

When the tabernacle was built, God specifically anointed Bezalel to create beauty in it: "to devise artistic designs, to work in gold, silver, and bronze, in cutting stones for setting, and in carving wood, to work in every craft."

God could have told them to simply build a big plain box. He could have only made it functional and practical. But He wanted the tabernacle to be beautiful to reflect His beauty.

The robes of the priests were also intended to be magnificent. Their purpose was "glory and beauty"!

> *And you shall make holy garments for Aaron your brother, for glory and for beauty. You shall speak to all the skillful, whom I have filled with a spirit of skill, that they make Aaron's garments to consecrate him for My priesthood. ... For Aaron's sons you shall make coats and sashes and caps. You shall make them for glory and beauty.* (Exodus 28:2-3, 40)

In the Temple of Solomon, there were two bronze pillars that stood on the porch:

> *He set up the pillars at the vestibule of the temple. He set up the pillar on the south and called its name Jachin, and he set up the pillar on the north and called its name Boaz.* (1 Kings 7:21)

These two pillars were very ornate and elaborate, and it seems that they were not support structures but were free-standing, with no apparent purpose other than being beautiful!

Just as God anointed Bezalel to create beauty in the Tabernacle of Moses, and just as Solomon created beauty in his temple, so we also should use God's gifts to create beauty through art, music, writing, architecture, gardening and other forms of creativity. Let us never be content with things that are merely functional but seek to honor the splendor of the preeminent Creator. And, as we do that, we must only do it to point people to Him – not to ourselves and not to the thing we made.

Above all, our lives should express the inner beauty of God's character – the true beauty.

> *... not pilfering, but showing all good faith, so that in everything they may adorn the doctrine of God our Savior.* (Titus 2:10)

When we live with good character and the fruit of the Spirit, our lives "adorn" the teaching of God!

> *... but let your adorning be the hidden person of the heart with the imperishable beauty of a gentle and quiet spirit, which in God's sight is very precious.* (1 Peter 3:4)

As we walk with God in union with Christ, our lives will be changed more and more into His image (2 Corinthians 3:18). Then, when Jesus returns, we will be to Him a splendidly beautiful Bride!

> *... so that He might present the Church to Himself in splendor, without spot or wrinkle or any such thing, that she might be holy and without blemish.* (Ephesians 5:27)

God desires His beautiful Bride, filled with character, faith, holiness, love for Him, worship of Him – a beautiful Bride for a beautiful God for a beautiful eternity!

<u>Transformational Implications:</u>

- Because God is beautiful, we will worship Him in the beauty of His holy Presence.

  > *Worship the Lord in the splendor of holiness; tremble before Him, all the earth!* (Psalm 96:9)

- Because God is beautiful, we will use His gifts to create beauty through art, music, writing, architecture, gardening and other forms of creativity so that we may honor the beauty and splendor of our magnificent Creator.

  > *So, whether you eat or drink, or whatever you do, do all to the glory of God.* (1 Corinthians 10:31)

- Because God is beautiful, as we live in union with Him, our lives should express the inner beauty of God's character – the true beauty.

  > *... but let your adorning be the hidden person of the heart with the imperishable beauty of a gentle and quiet spirit, which in God's sight is very precious.* (1 Peter 3:4)

God Is Light

God Is Light

> *This is the message we have heard from Him and proclaim to you, that God is Light, and in Him is no darkness at all.* (1 John 1:5)

God is not "a light" out of many other lights. He Himself is "Light." This is an aspect of His infinite Being as Spirit. He is pure, uncreated Light.

When Jesus came to the earth, He revealed the true, eternal Light of God.

> *The true Light, which gives light to everyone, was coming into the world.* (John 1:9)
>
> *Again Jesus spoke to them, saying, "I am the Light of the world. Whoever follows Me will not walk in darkness, but will have the light of life."* (John 8:12)
>
> *I have come into the world as Light, so that whoever believes in Me may not remain in darkness.* (John 12:46)

Indeed, Jesus Himself will be the Light of the eternal city of God:

> *And the city has no need of sun or moon to shine on it, for the glory of God gives it Light, and its Lamp is the Lamb.* (Revelation 21:23)

In eternity, there will be no need for electricity or light bulbs, or even the sun and moon. We will be bathed in the Light of the glory of God!

When referring to God, Light signifies at least two specific things: Truth and moral purity. Light is the opposite of darkness. Regarding both Truth and moral purity, God has no darkness in Him at all.

First, light signifies Truth. Light is visible, and it makes other things visible. When light shines in a room it makes everything visible. God's nature is such that He makes Himself known, and through the knowledge of God the true nature of everything else is revealed.

> *But when anything is exposed by the light, it becomes visible ... (Ephesians 5:13)*

Thus "Light" here signifies Truth. God is Truth and in Him there is nothing false. Moreover, His Light exposes the darkness, His Truth exposes the lies.

Second, "Light" also has a moral dimension. God is holy and in Him there is no moral darkness at all.

Because God is Light, those who are born of Him and know Him have been called out of the darkness and will walk in both Truth and holiness.

> *You are the light of the world. A city set on a hill cannot be hidden. Nor do people light a lamp and put it under a basket, but on a stand, and it gives light to all in the house. In the same way, let your light shine before others, so that they may see your good works and give glory to your Father who is in heaven. (Matthew 5:14-16)*
>
> *While you have the Light, believe in the Light, that you may become sons of Light ... (John 12:36)*
>
> *... for at one time you were darkness, but now you are light in the Lord. Walk as children of Light. (Ephesians 5:8)*

Just as Jesus is the Light of the world, He also told us that we are "the light of the world." This is because we have been born of Him and have His nature within us. Therefore, the truth and holiness of our lives will be seen by everyone around us; we will bring light and life to those around us.

Because we are children of Light, we must live in truth and holiness:

> *For you are all children of Light, children of the day. We are not of the night or of the darkness. So then let us not sleep, as others do, but let us keep awake and be sober.* (1 Thessalonians 5:5-6)
>
> *But you are a chosen race, a royal priesthood, a holy nation, a people for His own possession, that you may proclaim the excellencies of Him who called you out of darkness into His marvelous Light.* (1 Peter 2:9)

In contrast, those who do not know God will run from the Light.

> *If we say we have fellowship with Him while we walk in darkness, we lie and do not practice the truth.* (1 John 1:6)
>
> *And this is the judgment: the Light has come into the world, and people loved the darkness rather than the Light because their works were evil. For everyone who does wicked things hates the Light and does not come to the Light, lest his works should be exposed. But whoever does what is true comes to the Light, so that it may be clearly seen that his works have been carried out in God.* (John 3:19-21)

The true God, who is Light, stands in vivid contrast to the idols of men. Man's idols represent gods that cheat and lie, gods that are immoral, gods that are vindictive towards men, gods that argue and fight among themselves – gods that are much like man himself.

But the true God is Light. He is all truth, all faithfulness, all wisdom, all goodness, all holiness and righteousness. In Him there is no deceit, no meanness, no darkness, no trickery, no evil. He is a God that can be absolutely trusted, honored and loved.

Transformational Implications:

- Because God is Light, we will seek to express His Truth and holiness at all times in our daily lives.

> *...for at one time you were darkness, but now you are light in the Lord. Walk as children of light.* (Ephesians 5:8)

God Is Truth

> *Jesus said to him, "I am the Way, and the Truth, and the Life. No one comes to the Father except through Me ..."* (John 14:6)

God is Truth. He is ultimate reality. He does not merely say truthful things, He Himself is Truth.

Consequently, everything He knows or thinks is true. He is "perfect in knowledge" (Job 37:16). His "understanding is beyond measure" (Psalm 147:5).

God is not wrong or deceived about anything. He never makes mistakes. Therefore, everything God says is truthful. He never lies – about anything. We can trust Him for everything!

> *... in hope of eternal life, which God, who never lies, promised before the ages began.* (Titus 1:2)

In Titus 1, Paul says that because God never lies, therefore we know we have eternal life. We have absolute assurance of this! John says the same thing:

> *I write these things to you who believe in the Name of the Son of God, that you may know that you have eternal life.* (1 John 5:13)

Because God is Truth, we know we have eternal life.

In contrast to God who is Truth, Jesus said this about the devil:

> *You are of your father the devil, and your will is to do your father's desires. He was a murderer from the beginning, and does not stand in the truth, because there is no truth in him. When he lies, he speaks out of his own character, for he is a liar and the father of lies.* (John 8:44)

Here Jesus emphasizes the profound contrast between God and the devil. Five times in this one verse, Jesus says that the devil is a liar!

- "does not stand in the truth"
- "there is no truth in him"
- "when he lies"
- "he is a liar"
- "the father of lies"

God's core nature is Truth; Satan's core nature is lying. We should remember this the next time we are tempted to tell a "little white lie"!

Because God is Truth and never lies, therefore His Word is true, and it is the final standard of truth. We can always trust His Word.

> *But You are near, O Lord, and all Your commandments are true.* (Psalm 119:151)
>
> *The sum of Your Word is truth, and every one of Your righteous rules endures forever.* (Psalm 119:160)
>
> *Sanctify them in the truth; your Word is Truth.* (John 17:17)

Since we love God who is Truth, we will seek to deeply know His Word and walk in its Truth.

> *Oh how I love Your Law! It is my meditation all the day.* (Psalm 119:97)

> *Jesus answered him, "If anyone loves Me, he will keep My Word, and My Father will love him, and We will come to him and make Our home with him ..."* (John 14:23)
>
> *Do your best to present yourself to God as one approved, a worker who has no need to be ashamed, rightly handling the Word of Truth.* (2 Timothy 2:15)

The Word of God is a magnificent expression of the Truth of God, and we should love it!

Also, we should protect the centrality of the Word of God in the Church against all intrusions from man's theories, traditions and speculations. We must resist those influences and remain fully dedicated to the Word of God.

Because God is Truth, He is also faithful.

> *Know therefore that the Lord your God is God, the faithful God who keeps covenant and steadfast love with those who love Him and keep His commandments, to a thousand generations ...* (Deuteronomy 7:9)
>
> *For I will proclaim the Name of the Lord; ascribe greatness to our God! "The Rock, His work is perfect, for all His ways are justice. A God of faithfulness and without iniquity, just and upright is He."* (Deuteronomy 32:3-4)

God's faithfulness means that He will always do what He has said and fulfill what He has promised.

> *God is not man, that He should lie, or a son of man, that He should change His mind. Has He said, and will He not do it? Or has He spoken, and will He not fulfill it?* (Numbers 23:19)

We can fully trust God, despite whatever circumstances or struggles we may face. He promised that He would never leave us nor forsake us (Hebrews 13:5).

> *But the Lord is faithful. He will establish you and guard you against the evil one.* (2 Thessalonians 3:3)
>
> *... and since we have a great Priest over the house of God, let us draw near with a true heart in full assurance of faith, with our hearts sprinkled clean from an evil conscience and our bodies washed with pure water. Let us hold fast the confession of our hope without wavering, for He who promised is faithful.* (Hebrews 10:21-23)

Both 2 Thessalonians and Hebrews were written to believers who were suffering severely for their faith. God promised to keep them both, and they could know that He would since He is faithful to keep His promises.

Because God is Truth, those who know Him will pursue Truth and walk in Truth.

> *O Lord, who shall sojourn in Your tent? Who shall dwell on Your holy hill? He who walks blamelessly and does what is right and speaks truth in his heart; who does not slander with his tongue and does no evil to his neighbor, nor takes up a reproach against his friend; in whose eyes a vile person is despised, but who honors those who fear the Lord; who swears to his own hurt and does not change; who does not put out his money at interest and does not take a bribe against the innocent. He who does these things shall never be moved.* (Psalm 15:1-5)

2 Corinthians has a lot to say about spiritual ministry and true leadership. At the heart of healthy leadership is integrity and truthfulness. Paul refused to lie or deceive.

> *But we have renounced disgraceful, underhanded ways. We refuse to practice cunning or to tamper with God's Word, but by the open statement of the truth we would commend ourselves to everyone's conscience in the sight of God.* (2 Corinthians 4:2)

Christian leaders must walk in truthfulness, and, of course, this is true for all of us!

> *Do not lie to one another, seeing that you have put off the old self with its practices and have put on the new self, which is being renewed in knowledge after the image of its Creator.* (Colossians 3:9-10)

Because we are born of the God who is Truth, we also will be truthful and faithful in our relationships with others. We will keep our word – even if that means loss for us.

> *... [a blameless man] swears to his own hurt and does not change;* (Psalm 15:4)

Moreover, we will tell others of God's faithfulness:

> *I will tell of Your Name to my brothers; in the midst of the congregation I will praise You: You who fear the LORD, praise Him! All you offspring of Jacob, glorify Him, and stand in awe of Him, all you offspring of Israel! For He has not despised or abhorred the affliction of the afflicted, and He has not hidden His face from him, but has heard, when he cried to Him.* (Psalm 22:22-24)

In these ways, we will be children of Light!

> *... that you may be blameless and innocent, children of God without blemish in the midst of a crooked and twisted generation, among whom you shine as lights in the world ...* (Philippians 2:15)

Transformational Implications:

- Because God is Truth, we will trust Him to keep us and to fulfill all His promises.

  > *Therefore let those who suffer according to God's will entrust their souls to a faithful Creator while doing good.* (1 Peter 4:19)

- Because God is Truth, we will seek to deeply know His Word and walk in its Truth.

> *Oh how I love Your Law! It is my meditation all the day.* (Psalm 119:97)

- Because God is faithful, we also will be faithful in our relationships with others. We will keep our word – even if that means loss for us.

> *... [a blameless man] swears to his own hurt and does not change;* (Psalm 15:4)

- Because God is faithful to us, we will tell others about His faithfulness.

> *I will tell of Your Name to my brothers; in the midst of the congregation I will praise You: You who fear the* LORD, *praise Him! All you offspring of Jacob, glorify Him, and stand in awe of Him, all you offspring of Israel! For He has not despised or abhorred the affliction of the afflicted, and He has not hidden His face from him, but has heard, when he cried to Him.* (Psalm 22:22-24)

God Is Wise

Wisdom is the ability to use knowledge well. We all know people who have a lot of knowledge in their heads, and yet they are not very wise in their lives, and, in the end, they fail. Thus, knowledge by itself is not enough; we must be able to use that knowledge in a way that is wise.

Because God is Light, He sees and knows everything perfectly. He knows exactly how to solve every problem and explore every opportunity. He not only has perfect knowledge, but He has perfect wisdom to apply that knowledge in the best ways possible. Thus, God does everything in perfect wisdom.

> *It is He who made the earth by His power, who established the world by His wisdom, and by His understanding stretched out the heavens. (Jeremiah 10:12)*

In the beginning, God made the entire universe in His great wisdom, and, ever since that time, He has overseen all things in His wisdom.

In His infinite wisdom, God always chooses the best goals and the best means to accomplish those goals. There may be times when we question the wisdom of God allowing certain things to happen in our lives. However, whether or not we understand the wisdom of everything He does and allows to happen does not change the fact of its perfect wisdom.

Because God is wise, He is never mistaken. We can trust what He allows in our lives, knowing that all of it will, in the end, be for our good and for His glory.

> *And we know that for those who love God all things work together for good, for those who are called according to His purpose.* (Romans 8:28)

This promise gives us such peace and security in the midst of the storms of life.

In some of the psalms, the psalmist begins by questioning God's wisdom or righteousness in allowing particular things to happen. But God is so gracious and patient toward him, gently leading him to the place where he ultimately recognizes God's wisdom in it all. God led Job through this same process (Job 38 – 42), and He will also lead us through this as well, as we listen to Him and surrender to Him.

God's purposes are always perfect because He is perfect and wise. God's wisdom is infinite.

> *Oh, the depth of the riches and wisdom and knowledge of God! How unsearchable are His judgments and how inscrutable His ways!* (Romans 11:33)

Paul says that God's judgments are "unsearchable" and His ways are "inscrutable." This means there are times when we will not understand what He is doing. But God expects us to trust Him anyway. In those times, He invites us to ask Him to help us understand it. In His great love He gives us His wisdom when we ask!

> *If any of you lacks wisdom, let him ask God, who gives generously to all without reproach, and it will be given him.* (James 1:5)

The context of James 1:5 is James' teaching about trials of various kinds.

> *Count it all joy, my brothers, when you meet trials of various kinds, for you know that the testing of your faith produces steadfastness. And let steadfastness have its full effect, that you may be perfect and complete, lacking in nothing. If any of you lacks wisdom, let him ask God, who gives generously to all without reproach, and it will be given him.* (James 1:2-5)

James says we should count it "all joy" when we go through trials because we know that God will use it ultimately for our maturity. Because this can be hard for us to understand, James encourages us to ask God for wisdom about it.

What a gift! If we ask Him, God will share His wisdom with us, and He promises to do so generously!

Transformational Implications:

- Because God is wise, He is never mistaken. We can trust what He allows in our lives, knowing that it all will, in the end, be for our good and for His glory.

  > *And we know that for those who love God all things work together for good, for those who are called according to His purpose.* (Romans 8:28)

God Is Holy

The second aspect of God as Light is moral purity. God is holy and in Him, there is no sin, no darkness.

This is one of the most commonly named attributes of God in the Bible. In both testaments, God is repeatedly described as being "holy."

> *Speak to all the congregation of the people of Israel and say to them, you shall be holy, for I the Lord your God am holy.* (Leviticus 19:2)
>
> *Exalt the Lord our God, and worship at His holy mountain; for the Lord our God is holy!* (Psalm 99:9)
>
> *And one [seraph] called to another and said: "Holy, holy, holy is the Lord of hosts; the whole earth is full of His glory!"* (Isaiah 6:3)

Isaiah 6 is the only place in the Bible where the seraphim are mentioned. It seems that they do not do anything other than crying out to one another about the holiness of God. They do this for all eternity, yet they never get bored or need a break. They constantly cry, "Holy, holy, holy is the Lord of hosts; the whole earth is full of His glory!" God is so infinitely holy that He deserves this. There are also four living creatures named in Revelation 4 that do a similar thing:

> *And the four living creatures, each of them with six wings, are full of eyes all around and within, and day and night they never cease to say, "Holy, holy, holy, is the Lord God Almighty, who was and is and is to come!"* (Revelation 4:8)

God is so holy that His Spirit is called the Holy Spirit!

The Hebrew word for "holy" is *qadosh* (קָדוֹשׁ). It has two broad senses. First, it means "consecrated" or "separated." Thus, God is holy in the sense of separate and other than everything else. The Levitical priests were holy in the sense of being separated from other activities and consecrated to God. The vessels in the Temple were holy – they were dedicated to the service of worship and could be used for nothing else!

Second, *qadosh* means morally pure – this is usually what people think "holy" means.

The Greek word for "holy" is *hagios* (ἅγιος) and it has the same two broad senses: separation and moral purity.

Both of these senses apply to God.

First, God is "separate." He is completely different from everyone and everything else. He is eternal, infinite, uncreated Spirit.

> *For thus says the One who is high and lifted up, who inhabits eternity, whose Name is Holy: "I dwell in the high and holy place, and also with him who is of a contrite and lowly spirit, to revive the spirit of the lowly, and to revive the heart of the contrite ..."* (Isaiah 57:15)

God is so different He is high and lifted up, inhabiting eternity. Amazingly, He welcomes the lowly into His Presence!

Second, God is morally pure. He is completely separate from sin. There is no darkness, no sin in Him at all. Moreover, He requires His people to be consecrated to Him and to be separate from sin also.

> *For I am the Lord your God. Consecrate yourselves therefore, and be holy, for I am holy. You shall not defile yourselves with any swarming thing that crawls on the ground. For I am the Lord who brought you up out of the land of Egypt to be your God. You shall therefore be holy, for I am holy.* (Leviticus 11:44-45)

Because God is holy, therefore, those who are consecrated to Him – those who are His – will also be holy. Because He is separate, we also are to be separate.

> *As obedient children, do not be conformed to the passions of your former ignorance, but as He who called you is holy, you also be holy in all your conduct, since it is written, "You shall be holy, for I am holy."* (1 Peter 1:14-16)

Peter affirms that because we are God's children, born of Him and sharing His nature, we should be like Him in holiness.

God is so holy that objects and places associated with Him become holy also.

> *Then He said, "Do not come near; take your sandals off your feet, for the place on which you are standing is holy ground."* (Exodus 3:5)
>
> *... the Lord said to Moses, "Go to the people and consecrate them today and tomorrow, and let them wash their garments and be ready for the third day. For on the third day the Lord will come down on Mount Sinai in the sight of all the people. And you shall set limits for the people all around, saying, 'Take care not to go up into the mountain or touch the edge of it. Whoever touches the mountain shall be put to death. No hand shall touch him, but he shall be stoned or shot; whether beast or man, he shall not live.' ..."* (Exodus 19:10-13)
>
> *And you shall hang the veil from the clasps, and bring the ark of the testimony in there within the veil. And the veil shall separate for you the Holy Place from the Most Holy.* (Exodus 26:33)

The Levitical priests, who represented God, were to be physically perfect (Leviticus 21:17-23), and ceremonially pure (Leviticus 21:1-15) to be able to do their work. Their physical perfection and ceremonial purity represented holiness.

> *They shall be holy to their God and not profane the Name of their God. For they offer the Lord's food offerings, the bread of their God; therefore they shall be holy.* (Leviticus 21:6)

The animals sacrificed were also to be physically perfect, without any blemish.

> *And he shall bring to the priest as his compensation to the Lord a ram without blemish out of the flock, or its equivalent, for a guilt offering.* (Leviticus 6:6)

Even after the animals were killed, any of the vessels that were used in their killing or cooking then became holy and had to either destroyed or cleaned:

> *Speak to Aaron and his sons, saying, "This is the law of the sin offering. In the place where the burnt offering is killed shall the sin offering be killed before the Lord; it is most holy. The priest who offers it for sin shall eat it. In a holy place it shall be eaten, in the court of the tent of meeting. Whatever touches its flesh shall be holy, and when any of its blood is splashed on a garment, you shall wash that on which it was splashed in a holy place. And the earthenware vessel in which it is boiled shall be broken. But if it is boiled in a bronze vessel, that shall be scoured and rinsed in water."* (Leviticus 6:25-28)

Everything around God cries holiness! Thus, as those who are born of Him, God's children are to share in His holiness.

> *For they disciplined us for a short time as it seemed best to them, but He disciplines us for our good, that we may share His holiness.* (Hebrews 12:10)
>
> *Strive for peace with everyone, and for the holiness without which no one will see the Lord.* (Hebrews 12:14)
>
> *No one born of God makes a practice of sinning, for God's seed abides in him; and he cannot keep on sinning, because he has been born of*

> *God. By this it is evident who are the children of God, and who are the children of the devil: whoever does not practice righteousness is not of God, nor is the one who does not love his brother.* (1 John 3:9-10)

Please notice our holiness is the direct result of Jesus living in us and through us by His Spirit. We are only holy because we are "born of God." Holiness in our lives is not the result of our own human effort but His indwelling life.

Thus, from our inward union with Christ, we are to be morally separate from the corrupting influences of the world:

> *Do not be unequally yoked with unbelievers. For what partnership has righteousness with lawlessness? Or what fellowship has light with darkness? What accord has Christ with Belial? Or what portion does a believer share with an unbeliever? What agreement has the temple of God with idols? For we are the temple of the living God; as God said, "I will make My dwelling among them and walk among them, and I will be their God, and they shall be My people. Therefore go out from their midst, and be separate from them, says the Lord, and touch no unclean thing; then I will welcome you, and I will be a Father to you, and you shall be sons and daughters to Me, says the Lord Almighty."* (2 Corinthians 6:14-18; *see also* Romans 12:1; 2 Corinthians 7:1)

As we daily walk in union with Christ, looking at Him, surrendering to Him, He will change us more and more into His own holy image.

> *And we all, with unveiled face, beholding the glory of the Lord, are being transformed into the same image from one degree of glory to another. For this comes from the Lord who is the Spirit.* (2 Corinthians 3:18)

Of course, this does not mean we will achieve sinless perfection in this life but that we will daily put off the old nature and put on the new, seeking to know God and to be like Him in every way.

> *Not that I have already obtained this or am already perfect, but I press on to make it my own, because Christ Jesus has made me His own.* (Philippians 3:12)

Because our infinitely holy God punishes sin with the eternal punishment it deserves, we will fear Him and turn away from evil.

> *And He said to man, "Behold, the fear of the Lord, that is wisdom, and to turn away from evil is understanding."* (Job 28:28)
>
> *Be not wise in your own eyes; fear the* LORD, *and turn away from evil.* (Proverbs 3:7)

The child of God will not try to see how much sin he can get away with, but rather he will run from sin! This must be especially true of leaders; when leaders fall into sin and get away with it, often the people follow them and become even worse (1 Corinthians 5:6)!

Moreover, the Church as a whole is to grow "into a holy temple in the Lord" (Ephesians 2:21) so that when Jesus returns, she will "be holy and without blemish" (Ephesians 5:27). And after that, everything on the earth will be "Holy to the Lord"!

> *And on that day there shall be inscribed on the bells of the horses, "Holy to the Lord." And the pots in the house of the Lord shall be as the bowls before the altar. And every pot in Jerusalem and Judah shall be holy to the Lord of hosts ...* (Zechariah 14:20-21)

What was once inscribed only on the garments of the high priest (Exodus 28:36; 39:30) will become the description of all that is associated with the people of God in all the earth. Everything will be separated from sin and set apart to the holy service of our holy God for all eternity!

Transformational Implications:

- Because God is holy, we shall be holy also!

> *As obedient children, do not be conformed to the passions of your former ignorance, but as He who called you is holy, you also be holy in all your conduct, since it is written, "You shall be holy, for I am holy."* (1 Peter 1:14-16)

- Because our infinitely holy God punishes sin with the eternal punishment it deserves, we will fear Him and turn away from evil.

  > *And He said to man, "Behold, the fear of the Lord, that is wisdom, and to turn away from evil is understanding."* (Job 28:28)

God Is Righteous and Just

God's righteousness is the expression of His holiness as He interacts with man. Because He is holy, He always does what is right.

> *Far be it from You to do such a thing, to put the righteous to death with the wicked, so that the righteous fare as the wicked! Far be that from You! Shall not the Judge of all the earth do what is just?* (Genesis 18:25)
>
> *The Rock, His work is perfect, for all His ways are justice. A God of faithfulness and without iniquity, just and upright is He.* (Deuteronomy 32:4)
>
> *Of a truth, God will not do wickedly, and the Almighty will not pervert justice.* (Job 34:12)
>
> *The Lord is righteous in all His ways and kind in all His works.* (Psalm 145:17)
>
> *"... but let him who boasts boast in this, that he understands and knows Me, that I am the Lord who practices steadfast love, justice, and righteousness in the earth. For in these things I delight, declares the Lord."* (Jeremiah 9:24)
>
> *And they sing the song of Moses, the servant of God, and the song of the Lamb, saying, "Great and amazing are Your deeds, O Lord God the Almighty! Just and true are Your ways, O King of the nations!*

> *Who will not fear, O Lord, and glorify Your Name? For You alone are holy. All nations will come and worship You, for Your righteous acts have been revealed."* (Revelation 15:3-4)

However, at times, God does not appear to be just in His dealings with man. Those who lead sinful lives are not always punished, and the righteous frequently seem to go unrewarded.

In Psalm 73, Asaph reflected on the prosperity of the wicked and wondered how a righteous God could allow this.

> *Truly God is good to Israel, to those who are pure in heart. But as for me, my feet had almost stumbled, my steps had nearly slipped. For I was envious of the arrogant when I saw the prosperity of the wicked.* (Psalm 73:1-3)

It was when he recognized their end that the problem was resolved. The wicked may live in peace and prosperity for a short time, but, in the end, they will be destroyed.

> *But when I thought how to understand this, it seemed to me a wearisome task, until I went into the sanctuary of God; then I discerned their end. Truly You set them in slippery places; You make them fall to ruin ... For behold, those who are far from You shall perish; You put an end to everyone who is unfaithful to You.* (Psalm 73:16-18, 27)

In contrast, Asaph, a righteous man, would be guided by God now and ultimately be received to eternal glory.

> *Nevertheless, I am continually with You; You hold my right hand. You guide me with Your counsel, and afterward You will receive me to glory.* (Psalm 73:23-24)

This must be our perspective. In this life, things that appear unjust frequently happen, but, in eternity, God's justice will be complete.

Because God is righteous, He will ultimately treat people according to what they deserve. This means He will punish sin. However, because He is also gracious and merciful, He provided a Substitute – His own perfect Son – to pay the penalty for our sins!

Paul describes this in Romans 3:

> *... for all have sinned and fall short of the glory of God, and are justified by His grace as a gift, through the redemption that is in Christ Jesus, whom God put forward as a propitiation by His blood, to be received by faith. This was to show God's righteousness, because in His divine forbearance He had passed over former sins. It was to show His righteousness at the present time, so that He might be just and the justifier of the one who has faith in Jesus.* (Romans 3:23-26)

When Jesus died to pay the penalty for our sins, it showed that God was truly righteous, because He gave appropriate punishment for sin, even though He forgives sinners at the same time. Thus, God is both "just and justifier."

In this way, the Cross gloriously exhibits the wisdom of God which devised a perfect plan for reconciling the requirements of God's justice with the desires of His mercy and love.

> *... [God] devises means so that the banished one will not remain an outcast.* (2 Samuel 14:14)

The greatest problem confronting God was not how to create a universe out of nothing, or how to raise the dead, but how He, an infinitely holy and righteous God, could justify ungodly sinners.

> *Truly I know that it is so: But how can a man be in the right before God?* (Job 9:2)

God could not ignore the fact that man is guilty, yet He desired to save man. He had to provide a way of salvation that would not overlook man's sins but would satisfy the demands of the broken law which required the death of the sinner.

No man could ever conceive of such a plan, but at the Cross, God fully satisfied the claims of His own justice while freely pardoning and justifying sinners. Justice and mercy kiss each other.

> *Steadfast love and faithfulness meet; righteousness and peace kiss each other.* (Psalm 85:10)

Transformational Implications:

- Because God is righteous, we will pursue righteousness and justice in our lives.

    > *Hate evil, and love good, and establish justice in the gate; it may be that the* LORD, *the God of Hosts, will be gracious to the remnant of Joseph.* (Amos 5:15)
    >
    > *Therefore, if anyone cleanses himself from what is dishonorable, he will be a vessel for honorable use, set apart as holy, useful to the master of the house, ready for every good work. So flee youthful passions and pursue righteousness, faith, love, and peace, along with those who call on the Lord from a pure heart.* (2 Timothy 2:21-22)

God is Glorious

To say that God is glorious means two things.

First, God's glory means the magnificent light that surrounds God's Presence. God's glory was, at times, directly revealed to people in both testaments.

> *Then Moses went up on the mountain, and the cloud covered the mountain. The glory of the Lord dwelt on Mount Sinai, and the cloud covered it six days. And on the seventh day He called to Moses out of the midst of the cloud. Now the appearance of the glory of the Lord was like a devouring fire on the top of the mountain in the sight of the people of Israel.* (Exodus 24:15-17)
>
> *... and while My glory passes by I will put you in a cleft of the rock, and I will cover you with My hand until I have passed by.* (Exodus 33:22)
>
> *And when the priests came out of the Holy Place, a cloud filled the house of the Lord, so that the priests could not stand to minister because of the cloud, for the glory of the Lord filled the house of the Lord.* (1 Kings 8:10-11)
>
> *Bless the Lord, O my soul! O Lord my God, You are very great! You are clothed with splendor and majesty, covering Yourself with light as with a garment, stretching out the heavens like a tent.* (Psalm 104:1-2)
>
> *Like the appearance of the bow that is in the cloud on the day of rain, so was the appearance of the brightness all around. Such was the appearance of the likeness of the glory of the Lord. And when I saw it, I fell on my face, and I heard the Voice of one speaking.* (Ezekiel 1:28)
>
> *He was still speaking when, behold, a bright cloud overshadowed them, and a Voice from the cloud said, "This is My beloved Son, with whom I am well pleased; listen to Him."* (Matthew 17:5)

> *And an angel of the Lord appeared to them, and the glory of the Lord shone around them, and they were filled with great fear.* (Luke 2:9)

There is nothing more beautiful than the glory of God. It is the perfection of splendor.

Second, "glory" also means honor. To be glorious means to be worthy of honor and praise.

God is infinite and perfect in all His attributes. Therefore, He is infinitely glorious. We will never exhaust the glory of God. Even in eternity, we will never fully comprehend it, and we will never give God enough praise for it.

> *I will extol You, my God and King, and bless Your Name forever and ever. Every day I will bless You and praise Your Name forever and ever. Great is the Lord, and greatly to be praised, and His greatness is unsearchable.* (Psalm 145:1-3)
>
> *... to the only God, our Savior, through Jesus Christ our Lord, be glory, majesty, dominion, and authority, before all time and now and forever. Amen.* (Jude 25)

We will never get tired of glorifying God. The more we praise Him, the more we will want to praise Him!

God's own glory is His purpose in all that He does.

> *For from Him and through Him and to Him are all things. To Him be glory forever. Amen.* (Romans 11:36)

The whole universe displays the greatness of God:

> *The heavens declare the glory of God, and the sky above proclaims His handiwork.* (Psalm 19:1)

That is the purpose for which the heavens were made – to declare the glory of God. God could have created just one solar system, or just one species of plant, or made everything just one color; but

He created an almost infinite series of galaxies, and a tremendous variety of plants, animals and everything else, for the simple purpose of glorifying Himself.

> *For by Him all things were created, in heaven and on earth, visible and invisible, whether thrones or dominions or rulers or authorities – all things were created through Him and for Him.* (Colossians 1:16)

God's judgment and punishment of sin glorifies Himself in His holiness, righteousness and power:

> *... Thus says the Lord God: "Behold, I am against you, O Sidon, and I will manifest My glory in your midst. And they shall know that I am the Lord when I execute judgments in her and manifest My holiness in her ..."* (Ezekiel 28:22)
>
> *For the Scripture says to Pharaoh, "For this very purpose I have raised you up, that I might show My power in you, and that My Name might be proclaimed in all the earth."* (Romans 9:17)

And His redemption of undeserving sinners glorifies His grace, mercy and love:

> *... He predestined us for adoption to Himself as sons through Jesus Christ, according to the purpose of His will, to the praise of His glorious grace, with which He has blessed us in the Beloved ... so that we who were the first to hope in Christ might be to the praise of His glory ... [the Holy Spirit] is the guarantee of our inheritance until we acquire possession of it, to the praise of His glory.* (Ephesians 1:5-6, 12, 15)

Everything Jesus did, He did for the glory of His Father:

> *... the One who seeks the glory of Him who sent Him is true, and in Him there is no falsehood.* (John 7:18)
>
> *I glorified You on earth, having accomplished the work that You gave Me to do.* (John 17:4)

Jesus was not only doing the work of the Father; He was intentionally glorifying Him.

In particular, Jesus' death on the Cross revealed the glory of God.

> *When He had gone out, Jesus said, "Now is the Son of Man glorified, and God is glorified in Him ..."* (John 13:31)

The Cross glorified God's righteousness and holiness by judging sin with the judgment it required. At the same time, the Cross glorified God's love, mercy and grace upon those who will be saved. And, of course, the Cross glorified His infinite wisdom that designed such a salvation.

Everything, ultimately, is for God's glory.

> *"Worthy are You, our Lord and God, to receive glory and honor and power, for You created all things, and by Your will they existed and were created."* (Revelation 4:11)

This does not make God egotistical or proud. Because He is perfect, there simply is no higher purpose than His glory. It is the greatest and most virtuous possible end of all things.

Jesus said that He came to reveal the Father's glory and then, amazingly, to give this glory to us so that we also can be a display of His glory to the world.

> *I glorified You on earth, having accomplished the work that You gave Me to do. And now, Father, glorify Me in Your own Presence with the glory that I had with You before the world existed ... All Mine are Yours, and Yours are Mine, and I am glorified in them.* (John 17:4-5, 10)
>
> *The glory that You have given Me I have given to them, that they may be one even as We are One ...* (John 17:22)

> *... so that through the Church the manifold wisdom of God might now be made known to the rulers and authorities in the heavenly places. This was according to the eternal purpose that He has realized in Christ Jesus our Lord ...* (Ephesians 3:10-11)

This is the eternal purpose of God for the Church, that we would reveal the wisdom of God to the rulers and authorities in the heavenlies. This is our calling now.

Therefore, everything we do should be for the glory of God.

> *... for you were bought with a price. So glorify God in your body.* (1 Corinthians 6:20)
>
> *So, whether you eat or drink, or whatever you do, do all to the glory of God.* (1 Corinthians 10:31)
>
> *But you are a chosen race, a royal priesthood, a holy nation, a people for His own possession, that you may proclaim the excellencies of Him who called you out of darkness into His marvelous light.* (1 Peter 2:9)
>
> *As each has received a gift, use it to serve one another, as good stewards of God's varied grace: whoever speaks, as one who speaks oracles of God; whoever serves, as one who serves by the strength that God supplies – in order that in everything God may be glorified through Jesus Christ. To Him belong glory and dominion forever and ever. Amen.* (1 Peter 4:10-11)

Truly, it is our honor and privilege to give God all the praise, all the honor, all the glory – for all eternity.

In any case, He will not share His glory with anyone else! He is the only One truly deserving of glory.

> *I am the Lord; that is My Name; My glory I give to no other, nor My praise to carved idols.* (Isaiah 42:8)

God is to be loved and served, not only supremely but exclusively!

So let our cry be that of the psalmist:

> *Not to us, O Lord, not to us, but to Your Name give glory, for the sake of Your steadfast love and Your faithfulness!* (Psalm 115:1)

Transformational Implications:

- Because God is glorious we will worship Him – now and for all eternity!

  > *Bless the Lord, O my soul, and all that is within me, bless His holy Name!* (Psalm 103:1)
  >
  > *And I heard every creature in heaven and on earth and under the earth and in the sea, and all that is in them, saying, "To Him who sits on the throne and to the Lamb be blessing and honor and glory and might forever and ever!"* (Revelation 5:13)

- Because God is glorious, we will glorify Him with every part of our lives!

  > *So, whether you eat or drink, or whatever you do, do all to the glory of God.* (1 Corinthians 10:31)
  >
  > *... as it is my eager expectation and hope that I will not be at all ashamed, but that with full courage now as always Christ will be honored in my body, whether by life or by death.* (Philippians 1:20)

Behold Your God!

> *Go on up to a high mountain, O Zion, herald of good news; lift up your voice with strength, O Jerusalem, herald of good news; lift it up, fear not; say to the cities of Judah, "Behold your God!"* (Isaiah 40:9)

This is our God. This is the God we serve. Truly there is no one like Him!

> *"O Lord, God of Israel, there is no God like You, in heaven above or on earth beneath, keeping covenant and showing steadfast love to Your servants who walk before You with all their heart ..."* (1 Kings 8:23)
>
> *It will be said on that day, "Behold, this is our God; we have waited for Him, that He might save us. This is the Lord; we have waited for Him; let us be glad and rejoice in His salvation."* (Isaiah 25:9)

He is a God who is eternal Spirit, self-existent, independent, invisible and constant.

A God who is infinite in Presence, knowledge and power.

A personal God of love, goodness, grace and beauty.

A God who is Light and Truth. A God who is wise, holy, and righteous.

A God of infinite glory.

And this is the God who calls us to experience Him, to love Him, to serve Him, to know Him!

> *And this is eternal life, that they know You, the only true God, and Jesus Christ whom You have sent.* (John 17:3)
>
> *And we know that the Son of God has come and has given us understanding, so that we may know Him who is true; and we are in Him who is true, in His Son Jesus Christ. He is the true God and eternal life.* (1 John 5:20)

This is the God who gives us the privilege of glorifying Him and enjoying Him forever!

Let us not settle for anything less.

Errors About Who God Is

Several errors and misconceptions have already been dealt with. We shall deal with a few more here.

Seeing God in Our Own Image

It is far too easy for us to understand God as simply a "big Man" – basically like us, except bigger.

When we do that, we end up with a God who is not big at all; in fact, He becomes very small and very limited. But God is not a man.

> *God is not man, that He should lie, or a son of man, that He should change His mind ...* (Numbers 23:19)

As eternal, infinite Spirit, His existence is fundamentally different from ours.

He has none of the limitations that we daily experience. We must be careful that, in our thinking, we do not limit Him to what we are used to.

> *But Jesus looked at them and said, "With man this is impossible, but with God all things are possible."* (Matthew 19:26)

Because God is not like man, and limited like man, He can do anything!

<u>Transformational Implications:</u>

- Because God is not small like us, we can rest in His greatness.
- Because God is not like us, we can trust Him to keep His promises.

- Because God is not limited like us, we can rely on Him to do great things.
- Because God is not like us, we should rejoice in the truth that He relates to us through the person of Jesus Christ!

Are We "Little Gods"?

It has become a popular idea that Christians are "little gods" able to do godlike things. This idea sounds very exciting and is based, partly, on a misinterpretation of Psalm 82:

> *I said, "You are gods, sons of the Most High, all of you ..." (Psalm 82:6; see also John 10:34)*

Because we are godlike, our words supposedly have creative power. Just as God spoke the universe into existence in the beginning, we too are able to speak things into existence now – whether it be our own healing or prosperity, or blessing for others.

The error of this idea is quickly seen in the fact that, in reality, we simply cannot do godlike things. Jesus said we cannot add a single hour to our life or change the color of even one hair on our head.

> *And which of you by being anxious can add a single hour to his span of life? (Luke 12:25)*
>
> *And do not take an oath by your head, for you cannot make one hair white or black. (Matthew 5:36)*

Clearly, we do not have creative power as God does. We are not little gods. Man is created. We are lesser than God and utterly and eternally dependent on Him for everything.

> *And He is before all things, and in Him all things hold together.* (*Colossians 1:17*)

In Psalm 82, the psalmist Asaph refers to earthly judges and administrators of God's Law who, in effect, stood in His place representing Him. Those men were not fulfilling their responsibilities properly but were showing partiality to the wicked. So, God holds them accountable and tells them:

> *"How long will you judge unjustly and show partiality to the wicked? Selah. Give justice to the weak and the fatherless; maintain the right of the afflicted and the destitute. Rescue the weak and the needy; deliver them from the hand of the wicked."* (Psalm 82:2-4)

They had represented God in their roles but now He was going to judge them for their lack of integrity.

When we read both verses 6 and 7, the meaning is clear:

> *I said, "You are gods, sons of the Most High, all of you; nevertheless, like men you shall die, and fall like any prince."* (Psalm 82:6-7)

They were not "little gods" at all, but men – as all of us are.

<u>Transformational Implications:</u>

- Because we are not "little gods," we are dependent on God for everything and can rest in His care. We don't have to worry about tomorrow!
- Because we are not "little gods," we must place vengeance in God's hands, trusting that He will see justice be done.
- Because we are not "little gods," we will humble ourselves under His mighty hand, in the fear of God.
- Because we are not "little gods," we will pray in humble submission to God's will and eternal purposes.

Universalism

The heresy of Universalism or Ultimate Reconciliation grows out of an unbalanced concept of the love of God. Universalism teaches that since God is love He will ultimately save all people and they will be reconciled to Him.

There are two broad divisions of Universalists: those who teach the ultimate salvation of all men, and those who teach the ultimate salvation of all created beings, including the devil, the fallen angels and the demons.

Because God is love, they say, He does not desire that any of His creatures suffer eternally, but the punishments of the wicked in hell are for remedial, disciplinary purposes, and will ultimately lead them all to repentance and reconciliation with God.

However, while God is infinite love, He is also infinitely holy and righteous. God's love cannot overrule His holiness and justice and save those who reject Christ. The love of God has provided a Substitute for us. We do not need to die in our sins. But if we reject His love, then we will fall under His eternal justice.

There are many clear statements in the Bible that directly contradict the heresy of Universalism.

> *For the gate is narrow and the way is hard that leads to life, and those who find it are few.* (Matthew 7:14)

Jesus said that in the end, there will be comparatively "few" who will be saved. Elsewhere, Jesus affirms that many will be lost.

> *You serpents, you brood of vipers, how are you to escape being sentenced to hell?* (Matthew 23:33)
>
> *And these will go away into eternal punishment, but the righteous into eternal life.* (Matthew 25:46)

Significantly, the Greek word for eternal, *aiōnios* (αἰώνιος), is used twice in Matthew 25:46 – once for eternal life and once for eternal punishment. Thus, the punishment of the lost is just as everlasting in duration as the life of the righteous.

> *Whoever believes and is baptized will be saved, but whoever does not believe will be condemned.* (Mark 16:16)
>
> *Whoever believes in the Son has eternal life; whoever does not obey the Son shall not see life, but the wrath of God remains on him.* (John 3:36)
>
> *Their end is destruction, their god is their belly, and they glory in their shame, with minds set on earthly things.* (Philippians 3:19)

Obviously, the doctrine of ultimate reconciliation is false.

The reality of the eternal punishment of the lost should give us a healthy fear of God. Moreover, this will motivate us to pray for the lost and to reach out to them with the Gospel. However, if we believe that everyone will ultimately be reconciled to God, there will be no urgency in taking the Gospel to the nations – what a profound error!

Transformational Implications:

- Because of God's infinite love *and* infinite justice, we will pray for God to send out workers into His harvest, and we will strive to reach the lost with the Gospel.
- Because of God's infinite love and infinite justice, we will live out our salvation with fear and trembling, knowing that sin separates fallen man from God.

"The God of the Old Testament Is Very Different from the God of the New Testament"

According to this popular misconception, the Old Testament God was a God of justice and wrath, while the New Testament God is a God of love and grace.

In reality, God is the same in both testaments. His holiness and wrath against sin are revealed in both testaments, and His love and mercy are, as well.

The Old Testament is not only about God's holiness and wrath, but it says much concerning God's love and mercy. For example:

> *The Lord is slow to anger and abounding in steadfast love, forgiving iniquity and transgression ...* (Numbers 14:18)

> *In all their affliction He was afflicted, and the Angel of His Presence saved them; in His love and in His pity He redeemed them; He lifted them up and carried them all the days of old.* (Isaiah 63:9)
>
> *You shall not take vengeance or bear a grudge against the sons of your own people, but you shall love your neighbor as yourself: I am the Lord.* (Leviticus 19:18)
>
> *"Hear, O Israel: The Lord our God, the Lord is One. You shall love the Lord your God with all your heart and with all your soul and with all your might.* (Deuteronomy 6:4-5)

This is where Jesus got His two "great commandments" of love from (Matthew 22:36-40): the Old Testament!

Likewise, the New Testament not only reveals God's love, but it also speaks clearly regarding His holiness and wrath against sin. For example:

> *No, I tell you; but unless you repent, you will all likewise perish.* (Luke 13:3)
>
> *... whoever does not obey the Son shall not see life, but the wrath of God remains on him.* (John 3:36)
>
> *Note then the kindness and the severity of God: severity toward those who have fallen, but God's kindness to you, provided you continue in His kindness. Otherwise you too will be cut off.* (Romans 11:22)
>
> *For we must all appear before the judgment seat of Christ, so that each one may receive what is due for what he has done in the body, whether good or evil. Therefore, knowing the fear of the Lord, we persuade others ...* (2 Corinthians 5:10-11)
>
> *It is a fearful thing to fall into the hands of the living God.* (Hebrews 10:31)
>
> *... for our God is a consuming fire.* (Hebrews 12:29)

While there is a progression of revelation and theological development from the Old Testament to the New, nevertheless, there is not a contradiction between the two. Rather, there is continuity. God's nature is the same for eternity.

Transformational Implications:

- Since God is the same in both testaments, we can trust Him to be both holy and merciful in our own lives.
- Because God is the same throughout the Bible, we can trust the whole of His Word.

Difficult Passages

Can We Understand God at All?

God is infinite, man is finite. God is Spirit, man is flesh. God is holy, man is sinful. Can we even begin to understand God at all? He is so utterly different from us!

On one hand, God is indeed incomprehensible.

> *Oh, the depth of the riches and wisdom and knowledge of God! How unsearchable are His judgments and how inscrutable His ways!* (Romans 11:33)

At the same time, God has revealed Himself – at least partially – to man. Thus, to the extent that God has revealed Himself, we can know Him!

> *The secret things belong to the Lord our God, but the things that are revealed belong to us and to our children forever, that we may do all the words of this law.* (Deuteronomy 29:29)

Moreover, He wants us to seek Him and find Him.

> *The God who made the world and everything in it, being Lord of heaven and earth, does not live in temples made by man, nor is He served by human hands, as though He needed anything, since He Himself gives to all mankind life and breath and everything. And He*

> *made from one man every nation of mankind to live on all the face of the earth, having determined allotted periods and the boundaries of their dwelling place, that they should seek God, and perhaps feel their way toward Him*[7] *and find Him. Yet He is actually not far from each one of us ...* (Acts 17:24-27)

And He promises to reward those who seek to know Him.

> *And without faith it is impossible to please Him, for whoever would draw near to God must believe that He exists and that He rewards those who seek Him.* (Hebrews 11:6)
>
> *... the Lord searches all hearts and understands every plan and thought. If you seek Him, He will be found by you ...* (1 Chronicles 28:9)
>
> *The Lord is near to all who call on Him, to all who call on Him in truth.* (Psalm 145:18)
>
> *You will seek Me and find Me, when you seek Me with all your heart.* (Jeremiah 29:13)
>
> *Draw near to God, and He will draw near to you ...* (James 4:8)

These are beautiful promises – that God will reveal Himself to us when we seek Him! Of course, our seeking of Him must be by His Word and Spirit and not through our own wisdom and understanding.

> *The natural person does not accept the things of the Spirit of God, for they are folly to him, and he is not able to understand them because they are spiritually discerned.* (1 Corinthians 2:14)

As we seek Him, He will reveal Himself more and more to us, but because He is infinite, we will never exhaust His beauty, wisdom and glory. For eternity, we will explore the nature of God!

---

7 In the Greek, the expression "feel their way toward" means "to feel around for, to grope for, to try to find." The sense is of someone feeling his way in a dark room.

Let this be our cry – to know Him, love Him and serve Him.

> *... that I may know Him and the power of His resurrection, and may share His sufferings, becoming like Him in His death ...* (Philippians 3:10)

Transformational Implications:

- Because God reveals Himself to us, we should draw near to Him and seek to know Him!
- Because God reveals Himself to us, we should avoid the philosophies of man that seek to explain God and, instead, study the Word of God by which God is truly revealed.

Matthew 5:48

> *You therefore must be perfect, as your Heavenly Father is perfect. (Matthew 5:48)*

This was the direct instruction of the Lord Jesus so we must take it very seriously indeed. However, what does this mean? Are we literally to pursue perfection – the same perfection that God has?

Elsewhere in the New Testament, it is clear that we will not actually achieve perfection in this life.

> *Not that I have already obtained this or am already perfect, but I press on to make it my own, because Christ Jesus has made me His own. (Philippians 3:12)*
>
> *If we say we have not sinned, we make Him a liar, and His Word is not in us. (1 John 1:10)*

Moreover, if we are honest with ourselves, we will quickly admit that all of us are exceedingly far from perfection in this life! It is after death that we will be "made perfect" (Hebrews 12:23).

It is helpful to think of Jesus' words in Matthew 5 indicating not the *degree* of character we are to achieve (that is, sinless perfection) but rather the *kind* of character we are to pursue.

Verse 48 comes after Jesus' many previous instructions to love our enemies, give to the needy, pursue inward purity, and so forth. In those ways, we are to be like God. We are to pursue His image in our lives. We are to pursue love, holiness, truth, righteousness, mercy, grace.

Perfectionism will never help us. If we think we have achieved it, then we are proud and self-deceived. If we think we can never achieve it, then we will be self-condemned and hopeless. Either way we lose!

Let us stand in the great grace of God and pursue His ways and His image in our lives. But let us not come under the cruel taskmaster of perfectionism.

Transformational Implications:

- Because we cannot ever attain God's perfection, we will not rely on our own works. Instead, we will abide in Him, resting in His grace as we pursue the image of God in our lives.
- Because we cannot ever attain God's perfection, we will not hold others to an impossible standard.

2 Peter 1:4

> *... by which He has granted to us His precious and very great promises, so that through them you may become partakers of the divine nature, having escaped from the corruption that is in the world because of sinful desire.* (2 Peter 1:4)

Peter tells us that we are "partakers of the divine nature." To what extent have we partaken in God's nature? As we have seen, we are certainly not infinite in power, knowledge or presence – we do not partake of those aspects of His nature.

Peter tells us in the second half of this verse what he means:

> *... having escaped from the corruption that is in the world because of sinful desire.* (2 Peter 1:4)

He is not referring to the nature of God's infinite Being, but to the qualities of His character.

In the following verses, Peter exhorts us to pursue these qualities in our own lives:

> *For this very reason, make every effort to supplement your faith with virtue, and virtue with knowledge, and knowledge with self-control, and self-control with steadfastness, and steadfastness with godliness, and godliness with brotherly affection, and brotherly affection with love. For if these qualities are yours and are increasing, they keep you from being ineffective or unfruitful in the knowledge of our Lord Jesus Christ.* (2 Peter 1:5-8)

Transformational Implications:

- Because God calls us to be like Him, we will strive to be like Him by the power of His indwelling Spirit.

The Wrath of God

Many people do not understand the wrath of God and they wonder why a God of infinite love gets so angry with men.

But God's wrath is not a transient emotion. It is not the result of God having a "bad day" or being temporarily upset with man. Rather, it is the natural and inevitable expression of God's infinite holiness and pure righteousness toward the sin of man.

> *For the wrath of God is revealed from heaven against all ungodliness and unrighteousness of men, who by their unrighteousness suppress the truth.* (Romans 1:18)

Sometimes people say that God is angry in the Old Testament and then loving in the New. However, the wrath of God is revealed in the New Testament just as it is in the Old.

> *Whoever believes in the Son has eternal life; whoever does not obey the Son shall not see life, but the wrath of God remains on him.* (John 3:36)
>
> *But because of your hard and impenitent heart you are storing up wrath for yourself on the day of wrath when God's righteous judgment will be revealed.* (Romans 2:5)
>
> *Put to death therefore what is earthly in you: sexual immorality, impurity, passion, evil desire, and covetousness, which is idolatry. On account of these the wrath of God is coming.* (Colossians 3:5-6; see also Romans 2:8; 5:9; 9:22; 1 Thessalonians 1:10; 2:16; 5:9; Revelation 6:16-17; 19:15)

The wrath of God seems like such a negative thing. However, think what God would be like if He did not hate and judge sin. He would be a god who either approved of sin, or at least was not greatly troubled by it. Such a god would not be worthy of being worshipped and served.

We feel grieved when we see people getting away with murder, or child abuse, or genocide, or human trafficking. Even unbelievers complain about this! They find fault with God for allowing those atrocities to continue, and yet the same people think that God should let everyone do whatever they want. Just as we need a human government that maintains law and order, and provides for public safety, we should also be glad that our good and wise God punishes evildoers.

The reality is that sin violates the infinite holiness of God and must be punished. It is appropriate that God hates sin.

> *... do not devise evil in your hearts against one another, and love no false oath, for all these things I hate, declares the Lord.* (Zechariah 8:17)
>
> *You have loved righteousness and hated wickedness; therefore God, your God, has anointed you with the oil of gladness beyond your companions.* (Hebrews 1:9)

As God's children, we also should hate sin.

> *O you who love the Lord, hate evil! ...* (Psalm 97:10)
>
> *Let love be genuine. Abhor what is evil; hold fast to what is good.* (Romans 12:9)

But even though He hates sin and will ultimately punish it with the punishment it deserves, God's infinite love is still seen in the fact that He Himself bore the penalty of our sin so that we would not have to!

God also continues to be patient toward the wicked, delaying His judgment so they can come to Him and be saved.

> *The Lord is not slow to fulfill His promise as some count slowness, but is patient toward you, not wishing that any should perish, but that all should reach repentance.* (2 Peter 3:9)

Rather than being upset about the wrath of God, it is more appropriate that we thank Him for the gift of salvation from His wrath. And we should praise Him that He will one day fully deal with sin and create a new heavens and new earth in which there will only be His holiness, purity and Truth.

> *But according to His promise we are waiting for new heavens and a new earth in which righteousness dwells.* (2 Peter 3:13)

Transformational Implications:

- Because the wrath of God is consistent with who He is, we will shun sin and treat it seriously.
- Because of God's wrath, we will praise and thank Him for His mercy toward us, while crying out to Him to bring salvation to the world.
- Because of God's wrath, we will plead with sinners to repent and turn to Him!
- Because of God's wrath, we will live with joy and peace knowing that regardless of what bad things are going on around us, God will one day create a new heavens and earth and deal with sin forever.

Does God Change His Mind?

Since God is constant and never changes, how do we understand the passages in Scripture where God seems to change?

For example, many times, God declared that He would judge someone and then, because of prayer or the people's repentance (or both), God "changed His mind" and did not bring the judgment He had said He would.

For example, in Exodus 32, God told Moses He would destroy His people:

> *And the Lord said to Moses, "I have seen this people, and behold, it is a stiff-necked people. Now therefore let Me alone, that My wrath may burn hot against them and I may consume them, in order that I may make a great nation of you."* (Exodus 32:9-10)

Moses then interceded effectively on the people's behalf:

> *But Moses implored the Lord his God and said, "O Lord, why does Your wrath burn hot against Your people, whom You have brought out of the land of Egypt with great power and with a mighty hand? Why should the Egyptians say, 'With evil intent did He bring them out, to kill them in the mountains and to consume them from the face of the earth'? Turn from Your burning anger and relent from this disaster against Your people. Remember Abraham, Isaac, and Israel, Your servants, to whom You swore by Your own self, and*

> *said to them, 'I will multiply your offspring as the stars of heaven, and all this land that I have promised I will give to your offspring, and they shall inherit it forever.'"* (Exodus 32:11-13)

As a result, God "relented" and did not destroy them:

> *And the Lord relented from the disaster that He had spoken of bringing on His people.* (Exodus 32:14)

There are other examples of this in the Bible that all seem to indicate that God changes His mind (for example, Genesis 6:5-7; 1 Samuel 15:11; 2 Kings 20:1-6; Jonah 3:10).

As we saw earlier, as men interact with God, His responses to them will change. This does not indicate a change of God's eternal, unchanging Being, but it is an expression of His mercy when people repent. Just as God is holy and punishes sin, God is also merciful and forgives sin upon repentance. Both are unchanging characteristics of God. Just as His holiness never changes, so His mercy never changes either.

The opposite is also true. When a righteous man sins, he then comes under the judgment of God. God no longer blesses him but punishes him.

> *But when a righteous person turns away from his righteousness and does injustice and does the same abominations that the wicked person does, shall he live? None of the righteous deeds that he has done shall be remembered; for the treachery of which he is guilty and the sin he has committed, for them he shall die.* (Ezekiel 18:24)

In reality, if God did not respond differently when people acted differently, then people's actions would make no difference to God, and He would not be the unchanging God of justice and mercy portrayed in the Bible.

Transformational Implications:

- Because our unchanging God is merciful, we will intercede on behalf of others.
- Because God is merciful, we will turn away from sin and lead holy lives, seeking to please God.

Are There Things that God Cannot Do?

Sometimes people ask questions like, "Can God create a stone so large that He cannot lift it?"[8] Such foolish questions obscure the fact that there are some significant things that God cannot do.

The reality is that God can do all things that are in harmony with His nature. Thus, God cannot do things that are not in harmony with His nature. He cannot deny Himself (2 Timothy 2:13), He cannot lie (Titus 1:2), He cannot sin (James 1:13), He cannot change (Malachi 3:6). He cannot undo what has happened in the past, although He can erase its effects. He cannot be cruel or uncaring. He cannot fail to do what He has promised. So, yes, there are some things that God cannot do.

---

8 The correct answer is that there is no limitation on how large a stone God can create, or how large a stone He can lift.

Transformational Implications:

- Because God is omnipotent, we will worship Him for His power!
- Because God can do everything, we will trust Him to do the impossible.
- Because God can do everything, we will never ask for things that would violate His will and character. On the other hand, we can pray with great confidence, knowing that God will always be faithful to His own nature!
- Because God can do only those things that are in harmony with His nature, we will trust Him to accomplish His good will in our lives and in the world.

"If God Is Truthful, Why Is He Said to Deceive People?"

In several places in the Bible, God is said to deceive people. For example:

> *Now therefore behold, the Lord has put a lying spirit in the mouth of all these your prophets; the Lord has declared disaster for you.* (*1 Kings 22:23*)
>
> *Astonish yourselves and be astonished; blind yourselves and be blind! Be drunk, but not with wine; stagger, but not with strong drink! For the Lord has poured out upon you a spirit of deep sleep, and has closed your eyes (the prophets), and covered your heads (the seers).* (*Isaiah 29:9-10*)
>
> *Therefore God sends them a strong delusion, so that they may believe what is false, in order that all may be condemned who did not believe the truth but had pleasure in unrighteousness.* (*2 Thessalonians 2:11-12*)

First, such Scriptures should be understood in light of the sovereignty of God.[9] From God's side, all things happen according to His will and purpose; thus, He is said to be the One who did it. However, from

9 For a complete study of the sovereignty of God, please see *God Is Sovereign* by Malcolm Webber.

man's side, he chooses to do what he wants to do and, at times, he chooses to believe a lie. This is his responsibility, not God's.

Second, when man chooses to believe a lie and hardens his heart against God, God can give him up to be further deceived (Romans 1:18-32), allowing Satan to blind his eyes and take him deeper into darkness. This is God's righteous judgment.

Transformational Implications:

- Because God does not deceive us, He can be trusted for all things.
- Because God does not deceive us, we will guard our hearts and minds, so that we will not believe the enemy's lies or allow our hearts to harden against God.
- Because continually resisting God's truth may result in our being "given over" to deception, we will instead earnestly cry out to God that we may receive the "love of the Truth" (2 Thessalonians 2:10) and obey it (1 Peter 1:22).
- Because God desires us to know the truth, we will submit our lives to Him to be conformed to His truth (John 14:6; Ephesians 4:15).

"Since God Is Jealous, Can We Be Jealous Also?"

God reveals Himself as a "jealous God" many times in the Bible.

> *You shall not bow down to [idols] or serve them, for I the Lord your God am a jealous God, visiting the iniquity of the fathers on the children to the third and the fourth generation of those who hate Me ...* (Exodus 20:5)
>
> *... (for you shall worship no other god, for the Lord, whose Name is Jealous, is a jealous God) ...* (Exodus 34:14)
>
> *For the Lord your God is a consuming fire, a jealous God.* (Deuteronomy 4:24; see also Deuteronomy 6:15; 29:20; 32:16, 21; Psalm 78:58; Nahum 1:2; Zephaniah 3:8; 1 Corinthians 10:22)

Such statements are "anthropomorphisms"[10] and express, in a humanly understandable way, God's zeal for the protection of His own glory. God intensely desires that man's worship be given only to Him and not to false gods. Of course, it is appropriate for God to be jealous for this since He alone is truly worthy of all worship and glory.

---

10 An "anthropomorphism" is the attribution of human characteristics to a non-human entity, especially God. The purpose of an anthropomorphism is to allow us to understand and describe God in a way that makes sense to us.

It is also appropriate for God's servants to be jealous over God's people as Paul was:

> *For I feel a divine jealousy for you, since I betrothed you to one husband, to present you as a pure virgin to Christ.* (2 Corinthians 11:2)

This is not, however, an endorsement of human jealousy, which is almost always a self-serving expression of pride or one's own possessiveness.

In contrast, God's jealousy is a very beautiful thing. He wants us all for Himself. He wants us to be fully devoted to Him. And, as Paul was, we should be jealous for the people of God that they are fully devoted to Him.

Transformational Implications:

- Since God alone is truly worthy of glory, we will seek His glory in all we do, and not our own.
- Since God is jealous for His people, we will be jealous for the holiness and health of His Bride, the Church.

Key Truths and Biblical Verses for Memorization

God Is Spirit

> *God is Spirit, and those who worship Him must worship in spirit and truth.* (John 4:24)

God is self-existent

> *God said to Moses, "I am who I am." And He said, "Say this to the people of Israel: 'I am has sent me to you.'"* (Exodus 3:14)

God is eternal

> *Before the mountains were brought forth, or ever You had formed the earth and the world, from everlasting to everlasting You are God.* (Psalm 90:2)

God is independent

> *... The God who made the world and everything in it, being Lord of heaven and earth, does not live in temples made by man, nor is He served by human hands, as though He needed anything, since He Himself gives to all mankind life and breath and everything.* (Acts 17:24-25)

God is invisible

> *To the King of the ages, immortal, invisible, the only God, be honor and glory forever and ever. Amen.* (1 Timothy 1:17)

God is constant

> *Every good gift and every perfect gift is from above, coming down from the Father of lights, with whom there is no variation or shadow due to change.* (James 1:17)

God Is Infinite

God is everywhere

> *Where shall I go from Your Spirit? Or where shall I flee from Your Presence? If I ascend to heaven, You are there! If I make my bed in Sheol, You are there! If I take the wings of the morning and dwell in the uttermost parts of the sea, even there Your hand shall lead me, and Your right hand shall hold me.* (Psalm 139:7-10)

God is all-knowing

> *... for whenever our heart condemns us, God is greater than our heart, and He knows everything.* (1 John 3:20)

God is all-powerful

> *Ah, Lord God! It is You who have made the heavens and the earth by Your great power and by Your outstretched arm! Nothing is too hard for You.* (Jeremiah 32:17)

God Is Love

> *Anyone who does not love does not know God, because God is love.* (1 John 4:8)

God is personal

> *If you then, who are evil, know how to give good gifts to your children, how much more will your Father who is in heaven give good things to those who ask Him!* (Matthew 7:11)

God is good

> *The Lord is good to all, and His mercy is over all that He has made.* (Psalm 145:9)

God is gracious

> *... so that you may be sons of your Father who is in heaven. For He makes His sun rise on the evil and on the good, and sends rain on the just and on the unjust.* (Matthew 5:45)

God is beautiful

> *One thing have I asked of the Lord, that will I seek after: that I may dwell in the house of the Lord all the days of my life, to gaze upon the beauty of the Lord and to inquire in His temple.* (Psalm 27:4)

God Is Light

> *This is the message we have heard from Him and proclaim to you, that God is Light, and in Him is no darkness at all.* (1 John 1:5)

God is truth

> *Jesus said to him, "I am the Way, and the Truth, and the Life. No one comes to the Father except through Me ..."* (John 14:6)

God is wise

> *It is He who made the earth by His power, who established the world by His wisdom, and by His understanding stretched out the heavens.* (Jeremiah 10:12)

God is holy

> *As obedient children, do not be conformed to the passions of your former ignorance, but as He who called you is holy, you also be holy in all your conduct, since it is written, "You shall be holy, for I am holy."* (1 Peter 1:14-16)

God is righteous and just

> *Far be it from You to do such a thing, to put the righteous to death with the wicked, so that the righteous fare as the wicked! Far be that from You! Shall not the Judge of all the earth do what is just?* (Genesis 18:25)

God Is Glorious

> *The heavens declare the glory of God, and the sky above proclaims His handiwork. (Psalm 19:1)*
>
> *I will extol You, my God and King, and bless Your Name forever and ever. Every day I will bless You and praise Your Name forever and ever. Great is the Lord, and greatly to be praised, and His greatness is unsearchable. (Psalm 145:1-3)*

Made in the USA
Monee, IL
09 September 2024

64963687R00098